The
SMALL BUSINESS
success
Guide

Margie Sheedy

Wrightbooks

First published 2010 by Wrightbooks
an imprint of John Wiley & Sons Australia, Ltd
42 McDougall Street, Milton Qld 4064

Office also in Melbourne

Typeset in Giovanni 10.5/12pt

© Margie Sheedy 2010

The moral rights of the author have been asserted

National Library of Australia Cataloguing-in-Publication data:

Author:	Sheedy, Margie.
Title:	The small business success guide / Margie Sheedy.
ISBN:	9781742169590 (pbk.)
Notes:	Includes index.
Subjects:	Small business—Management. Success in business.
Dewey Number:	658.022

Cover design by Xou Creative

Cover image © iStockphoto/Hamster3d

Information on pp. 176–179 sourced from the Australian Taxation Office website <www.ato.gov.au> copyright Commonwealth of Australia, reproduced with permission.

Printed in China by Printplus Limited

10 9 8 7 6 5 4 3 2 1

Disclaimer
The material in this publication is of the nature of general comment only, and does not represent professional advice. It is not intended to provide specific guidance for particular circumstances and it should not be relied on as the basis for any decision to take action or not take action on any matter which it covers. Readers should obtain professional advice where appropriate, before making any such decision. To the maximum extent permitted by law, the author and publisher disclaim all responsibility and liability to any person, arising directly or indirectly from any person taking or not taking action based upon the information in this publication.

Contents

Part V: nutting out the legals and logistics

Part VI: growing, growing, gone?

About the author

© Kristy White

Margie Sheedy is an experienced journalist with a 20-plus-year media career under her belt. She has launched national magazines, been a senior editor and now writes extensively for newspapers, magazines and online sites. She thrives on finding practical information, and presenting it in a dynamic, easy-to-understand way. This is a hallmark of her style. Having created a successful freelance business which she juggles with the demands of a young family, Margie knows the thrills and challenges of running her own show. Along the way she also has set up and sold another ongoing wholesale small business. She is inspired by the idea that there must be better ways to do things, which led her to research and write this book.

Acknowledgements

There are many people who have helped make this book possible. Firstly, I would like to express my sincere thanks to the many business experts and government departments for giving me approval to share their ideas and information with you. Their information has made this book a credible resource. In particular, I would like to thank my 'brains trust' for giving up their valuable time and sharing their insights during extensive interviews: Dr Graham Godbee of Terris Business Consulting, lecturer at Macquarie Graduate School of Management and author of *Manage for All Seasons*; Kathryn Conder, partner of executive and business mentoring firm Carnegie Management Group; Haydn Thomas, chief executive of HIT Consulting; Associate Professor Isabel Metz, associate professor of organisational development at Melbourne Business School; Professor Ian Williamson, professor of management at Melbourne Business School; Michelle Gamble, founder and director of Marketing Angels; Frank Brass, regional director of national tax accountant firm H&R Block; Sharri Boucher founder of Jakiti Design; Dr Maree Bernoth, an OH&S researcher and lecturer at Charles Sturt University; Avron Newstadt, principal con-sultant with Expense Reduction Analysts; and Professor Beth Walker, director of the Small and Medium Enterprise Research Centre, Edith Cowan University.

Most importantly, I want to thank my husband Haydn for his encouragement and support at every turn, and my gorgeous children, Lauren, Justin and Amber, who inspire me every day.

Introduction

Owning a small business is a spectacularly individual adventure. Your efforts span all industries (representing 96 per cent of all business[1]), geographical locations and operational sizes, from sole traders and micro businesses of one or two people through to the Australian Taxation Office's definition as a business with fewer than 20 employees. You have different levels of entrepreneurial experience and gauges of success from the small business owner next to you. You might already have a successful small business, or be looking to start a new adventure. Either way, you've picked up *The Small Business Success Guide* because you believe there might be a few things you could do better or smarter. Your questions about business form the basis of this book. The answers are presented to you in easily digestible parts, complete with lots of ideas to action.

---

[1] The Australian Bureau of Statistics, *Counts of Australian Businesses, including Entries and Exits* report, June 2003 to June 2007, cat. 8165.0.

The reality for you and the 1.93 million other small business operators in Australia is that being in business for yourself isn't always easy[2]. You're expected to know a lot about everything, often straight away. Sure you have the flexibility and freedom of running your own show. But you also have all the frustrations and stresses. You might be a wonderful technician and know a lot about your industry or have the best money-making idea, but you may not have had to manage customers, suppliers or staff before. You might be fantastic with financials, but when it comes to marketing, it's all a blur of mixed messages. Add to that an ever-changing external business world and it's no wonder you might refer to your small business as the wildest ride of your life.

For advice, you rely on friends, family and associates who may have or do run their own businesses. However, there's an old cliché that might be worth remembering: 'you know what you know'. This is particularly apt when it comes to small business. People are happy to give you guidance. In fact, it seems everyone's an expert when it comes to your business. However, depending on the person's background and personal journey, they may be an expert only within the realms of their own experience.

The Small Business Success Guide strives to broaden your knowledge base. The information within these pages comes straight out of the mouths of some of Australia's leading small business experts, and from reputable government publications and online sites (with direct reference links). Think of them as your brains trust. You'll read about the highs and lows of small business, and discover some backed-by-research strategies to try out yourself. Having run my own small freelance business for many years, and set up and sold another ongoing small business along the way, I know how frustrating it can be to

---

[2] The Australian Bureau of Statistics, *Counts of Australian Businesses, including Entries and Exits* report.

be in the throes of success and then realise you need more information. You're kicking around as many balls as you can, but you don't have time to look up and work out the direction of the goal. This book will hopefully give you some direction. Like any good coach, its aim is to celebrate your achievements while showing you some shortcuts to sustainable success.

Some of the information you read here could be things you already know. Other ideas will be new. Others will put into question how you do things. If, by reading this book, you simply look more critically at your business, your purchase has been worthwhile. And if any of the techniques in *The Small Business Success Guide* help you fast-track your success, then it has succeeded in its endeavour. Good luck!

Part I

Getting the basics right

This first part is all about you. It aims to help you unravel some of the personal and professional quandaries that come with being a small business owner. While every business is different, and you know your business better than anyone, true success happens when you can tap into your strengths and work smarter, not harder.

Many top small businesses put their success down to a mixture of luck and good management. Being lucky is about opening yourself up to opportunities. Good management is having the knowhow, and the capacity, to jump on them at the right time. In the end, both come down to your ability to turn a vision into a workable, and profitable, reality.

1

Question: *What's the number one key to small business success?*

Answer: *It's all about you as the driver of your business.*

Small business starts with you in the driver's seat. You're the one with the ideas. You're the one with the vested interest. However, to be a truly successful small business owner, it's not enough just to be in charge of the steering wheel. You need a vision for where you want to go in your business, and a strategy of how you're going to get there. You can run your business without these things, but it's going to be a bumpier ride than it needs to be.

Researching success

There's been a lot of research worldwide on why some small businesses are more successful than others. According to Professor Beth Walker, director of the Small and Medium Enterprise Research Centre (SMERC) at Edith Cowan University in Western Australia, the key ingredient is strategic planning. For the majority of small business owners, thinking strategically is something they just don't do. The reason, she suggests, comes down to your motivation for getting into business in the first place.

'The literature suggests that individuals are either "pulled" or "pushed" into business', states Professor Walker. 'A "pull" motivation is an individual's positive inner desire to start a business venture and is centred on the potential new business owner's need to take control and change his or her work status as an "employee".' She says that 'pull' factors include wanting to be your own boss, the desire to create your own wealth and the need for a lifestyle change. 'Push' motivations, on the other hand, can include job frustration and a current lack of opportunities, wanting to escape from being continually supervised and even the threat of unemployment or retrenchment.

Meaningful motivation

Walker says that while small business ownership is often a mix of 'push' and 'pull' factors, her research indicates that some of these motivations leave you better equipped to manage your business than others. 'In most cases, operators in business to achieve financial goals were more likely to engage in strategic planning than operators motivated by lifestyle change and those "pushed" into small business ownership', says Walker. 'Operators driven by personal achievement goals were similar to "financial" operators and showed a greater likelihood to strategically plan.' This planning process involved having a formal (written) short- and long-term plan, and then dedicating time to review the plan. 'Given that strategic planning is a vital part of business success, it is reasonable that operators motivated by financial goals would engage in such planning to improve the performance of their businesses', she adds.

The good news is that, regardless of your motivation, it's never too late, or early, to instigate strategic thinking into your business. You can be more resourceful and open yourself up to different ways of running things, many of which are covered in this book. By taking control of what you do *and* how you do it, you can make even the best small business idea even more successful.

Action item: write it down

Keeping a daily or weekly journal helps get your thoughts, your business satisfactions and stresses out of your head. It doesn't have to be *War and Peace*. Just by jotting down a few happenings from the day, you'll be surprised how well you suddenly sleep at night. Keep your journal next to your bed just in case you do wake up thinking about work in the middle of the night. Write it all down. It'll take a lot of the emotion out of any dramas in your day, and give you the chance to celebrate even your smallest wins.

Taking control

One of the biggest challenges in small business is you. You don't always give yourself the credit you deserve. You love getting your hands dirty but can get so immersed in the operational side of things that you don't have time to plan long term. And you often don't give yourself a break when any stresses start to build. Here are some ways to steer yourself smoothly through the following situations:

→ *Daily dramas.* Sometimes it feels like you spend the whole day chasing your tail. You don't want to complain because times are good. However, if you don't get some of your business processes sorted at a strategic level, it won't take much to tip you out of control. It could be something as simple as streamlining your bookkeeping processes so that you're always on top of your cash flow. Or ordering supplies sooner so that production doesn't back up. Or working out why a client or staff member is being difficult, and how you should react. Daily dramas will happen. However, by spending a bit of time on how you do things, you'll be able to stay in control.

→ *Working around the clock.* The reality of running a small business is that you do take on a lot. You wade into the paperwork when you get home, and spend hours trying to manage your cash flow (more on this in question 10). It's no wonder you sometimes feel overwhelmed. But it's important to put a price on your own sanity. If you got sick, would your business still succeed? Rather than believing you need to work around the clock to be success-ful, allocate some of your time to your own physical and mental wellbeing. Take that lunch break. Do some exercise before or after work. Meet a friend for a drink. The healthier your mind and body are from the outset, the easier you'll cope with what's being thrown at you.

→ *It's lonely at the top.* Because you're running things, there aren't a lot of people off whom you can bounce the not-so-smooth parts of your business. Your life partner might be sympathetic and supportive, but mightn't be able to offer any solutions. Or he or she could be in the business with you, and be feeling just as frustrated. However, there are 1.93 million other small business owners in this country who share similar highs and lows, according to the latest data from the Australian Bureau of Statistics. Your job is to find just one set of these sympathetic ears. They might have some suggestions, or simply offer you some support because they know what you're going through. Remember, stress is a reality of life whether you're in small business or not. And talking about any dramas can put everything into perspective. The great thing about running your own show is that you have the power to make your small business life as great as it can be. So start exerting your influence on yourself today.

Strategic thinking tips

Thinking strategically is all about considering the big picture, knowing where you want your business to go and how this all fits together. It doesn't have to be convoluted, but it does have to be regular. Here are six strategic questions that can get you started:

- Who are my customers?
- What products or services do they want to buy and what are my competitors offering?
- When do they want these products or services: daily, weekly, monthly, seasonally, yearly?
- Where are my customers located?
- Why would they buy these products or services?
- How do I provide the products or services and how do I deliver on my customers' expectations?

2

Question: *I'm wearing so many hats: how do I keep it all in perspective?*

Answer: *By realising you can't always do everything.*

You've probably worked for someone else at some point in your life. You may have even worked in a large business where there were people to do everything: from the accounts to the hiring and firing to the packing of boxes. Now that you own your own small business, it's a different story. You don't have a lot of manpower, so you end up wearing many different hats, often at the same time. You're head of sales, marketing, production and customer service accounts. You hire staff, do the Business Activity Statements (BAS) and organise your own business trips, as well as all the other things that go into making a small business tick. 'Small business owners are the same as general managers in large organisations', says Associate Professor Isabel Metz of Melbourne Business School. By definition, a general manager has a broad cross-sectional understanding of the business he or she manages. This is what the small business owner has. The difference is that the general manager progresses through a career, adds Metz. 'They have had the time to attain the experience or education, whereas as a small business owner you may not have had the time to acquire the different functions. You learn as you go.' This learning process is driven by your business growth: you do a heap of different things at the start, and take on even more responsibilities as you get more successful. But rather than throwing some of your old hats back onto the rack, you try to keep doing all the things you've always done. That's where the stress of wearing so many hats hits home. The good news is it's never too late to get it all in perspective.

Direct your troops

Stop thinking of yourself as the only one who can do things in your business. Sure, you need to know about every part of your operation, but that doesn't mean you have to do it all, too. Start leading your troops (even the other people and businesses you get to do work for you). It's an important change of mindset, but one that successful small business owners do early on in their business's growth. 'It's about harnessing efforts, knowledge and action to your small business goals', says Metz.

Value your time

Look at what you do every day in terms of an hourly rate. If someone asked you to do a job, what would you charge yourself out at? Then take this rate and apply it to everything you do through the day. Think of yourself as the brain surgeon of your business: you're the one who works the miracles and follows up with great customer service after the operation. Is your business paying a brain surgeon to prep the operating theatre, set out the scalpels and clean up afterwards? Start valuing your time by looking at it in terms of your bottom line. Should you be doing something else that will actually benefit your business's potential?

Learn to delegate

As the brain surgeon, who could you delegate other tasks in your business to? If your answer is, 'there is no-one', you might still be in the set-up phase of your business. That's okay, as long as you have a vision for how you will run things when your business starts to grow. A lot of small business owners come unstuck in their development (and prosperity) because they continue to think that they're the only ones who can pack the boxes, answer the phones and do the mail run. You might need to pay someone to do some of this, but it will free you up to spend your energy *on* your business, rather than *in* your business.

Plan your day

The other way to take some of the stress out of your juggling act is to allocate time to various tasks. Rather than swapping hats when people ring for an accounts query, tell them you'll get someone to call them back. It may even be you. The benefit is that you can allocate a time in your day to do it. Every 10 or 15 minutes it takes you to follow things up is 10 or 15 minutes you're not working on your business. And if you try to do lots of things at once, nothing will be done properly. So plan your day in chunks of time, write it down and stick to your schedule, not someone else's. Keep in mind what you want to achieve each day and your juggling act won't seem so daunting.

Time management tips

- Say 'no' to the things that really can wait. If that means letting a call go through to the answering machine when you're in the middle of something, then so be it.

- Keep your diary up to date and note any changes to appointments and meetings as soon as they happen.

- Do things right the first time.

- Handle each piece of paper only once.

- Set your priorities for the day and the week. Then tick them off as you achieve them. This helps you stay focused, and reminds you to give yourself a pat on the back.

Be aware of stress

Stress is basically your body reacting to a situation you're not totally comfortable with. What triggers it is different for everyone. The key is to recognise how it affects you physically. Maybe you're not sleeping as well as you used to. You've started getting headaches. You start eating too much, or drinking or smoking more as a way to cope. You lose your temper easily. Basically, you feel strung out. However, you didn't start your small business to end up as a health statistic! When things feel a bit out of control, make a conscious effort to stop, take a deep breath and calmly try to think of a way to get it all sorted. If this means getting out of the office for a few minutes to clear your head, it's time well spent.

Stick to your vision

Wearing multiple hats is exhilarating when you start a business. For the first time in your working life you're in control of your own destiny. But it doesn't take long for the novelty to wear off and the pressure to build. That's when it's a good idea to reconnect with your business vision. 'Vision is linked to the strategy and the plans that are in place', says Metz. 'It creates a culture that glues your business together.' While you have the ultimate responsibility for the decisions made, you should trust others, delegate as much as you can and become an overseer so that you're not wearing so many hats at one time. This is exactly what the most successful leaders do.

3 **Question:** *Which ideas will make me the most money?*

Answer: *Ideas that are driven by passion and backed by research always have a better chance.*

Ideas, vision and the entrepreneurial spirit are the seeds from which small business grow. But like any seed, it's handy to know what you're dealing with before you plant it. Try visualising your idea. How big is it? How robust does it look? How big will it grow? How big do you *want* it to grow? Once you have the look and feel of it firmly in your mind, picture who else will appreciate its beauty. Would they pay good money for it? How do you know? Some ideas are more commercial than others. The trick is to know a bit about its potential before you dig the hole.

Commercial feasibility

If your new product or service idea didn't exist, would anybody notice? Kathryn Conder, partner of executive and business mentoring firm Carnegie Management Group, advises against the easy option of asking your family and friends what they think. 'Either they will agree with you that it's a great idea because they believe in you, or they'll try to discourage you and question everything about the idea, without thinking about the things they should be asking you', she says. Instead, talk to other people you respect who have experience in small business and have done it well; they're usually happy to share what's worked and what hasn't in their businesses. Conder says it's simply worth seeing what they think: it could save you a lot of time and heartache.

To give your idea a better chance of commercial success, the Queensland Department of Employment, Economic Development and Innovation <www.business.qld.gov.au> suggests you spend the time to consider: the trends in your industry; whether the industry is growing or slowing; the profile (age, sex and income) of the people you think you'll be selling the idea to; how many competitors you'll have; where your suppliers are (and any logistics issues); and how buoyant the local economy is.

'Unless the idea is going to turn a profit, why are you doing it?' asks Conder. Have you done some forecasts of what it's going to cost you to take the idea to market? How big is the market of willing purchasers? 'If there's no market out there, or if the cost of getting it to your market is far greater than people are prepared to pay, you have a problem', says Conder.

Action item: feasibility study

You probably have lots of ideas in your business, but not all of them will be commercially viable. A feasibility study can help you work out which ideas have better legs than others. Feasibility studies are all about putting your ideas on paper and then weighing up how you will make each one happen. The State Library of Queens-land offers a good feasibility study template to get you going (you'll find the PDF template at <www.slq. qld.gov.au/info/bus/sb/feasibility>). Grab a piece of paper and start writing!

Do your homework

Check with the Australian Bureau of Statistics <www.abs. gov.au>, which has a lot of free online information on people, including where they live, what they do, how they spend their money and whether or not they use the internet. Then start investigating what else you can find out about your potential customers. (For tips on doing market research that means something, see question 27). Take the time to do as much research as you can. As part of your quest, talk to a business expert or two. You could start with the free advice offered by a Business Enterprise Centre (BEC), which is a national network that offers small business advice (check out the website <www.beca.org.au>). Then there are industry organisations that are more than happy to share their perception of what's going on in your sector. They also can give you some idea of the capital expenses you'll need to cover, such as the cost of any plant and equipment, and ballpark figures for working capital so you can easily manage to pay for producing an idea, getting it to market, and keeping it there until your business can sustain itself with your own cash flow (for more on this, see question 10).

The time is right

Getting the timing right for a new idea is critical. 'If your idea is good but you're five years out from when the market will be ready to pay for it, your business will be incredibly hard work', says Conder. If you already have products and services out there, do some regular business navel-gazing. Has your market changed? Are people viewing your product differently? Is this affecting their purchasing power? Things can change quickly in a market, and you don't want to be left on the shelf.

Conder says you only have to think back to the first half of 2007, when there was a huge influx of senior citizens going online for the first time, to see how you can ride a wave or be dumped. Seniors realised that the internet could actually make their lives easier, and that they could go online to do their banking safely and securely. That opened the floodgates: the internet suddenly became a credible marketing and sales tool with seniors. 'Anyone who had this group in their market segment, and didn't realise this opportunity for growth, was left behind', she says.

If your industry is fast-paced and you need to make a decision on a new idea in a short time frame, you might have to work smarter, not harder. You could get connected to your target market via the various online social networking sites they enjoy (see more details on social media in question 30) and ask people what they think. Just be prepared for some honest answers. And before you go into an online forum to validate your idea (or you're thinking you might launch it as an online business), first get your website up to scratch. The people who respond to your online queries *will* go to your site to check what your business is about and how professional it is.

Find out ways to have what Conder calls 'continual communication': get your market to tell you what they want, and how you can give it to them. 'While there are no guarantees, the information you have, along with your passion, perseverance and drive, will then fuel your business's growth.'

Question: *Which survival strategies will help my business through tough times?*

Answer: *The best strategies get you to take a good hard look at the status quo.*

When times are tough, the tough get going. And it's no different in your business. Sometimes there'll be periods when things don't go exactly to plan. Maybe an order you were counting on has fallen through. Or your debtors are refusing to pay you what they owe. Or your production has ramped up but you don't have the cash reserves to pay for it. The list goes on. But for every testing time, there's a proven strategy that can help you survive in the short term and thrive when things turn around.

Dr Graham Godbee, author of *Manage for All Seasons* and a lecturer with the Macquarie Graduate School of Management, calls it 'the triage strategy'. Basically, you address the worst injuries first. 'Do you have internal bleeding or do you just need some cosmetic surgery?' he asks. What's caused the injury, and can you fix it? First up, he always advises small business owners to look at their cash flow. It will give you a good indication of where you're at, and how much time you have before a stretched situation gets more serious.

If you're in trouble with cash flow (more on this in question 10), he suggests quickly going through your product lines. 'Think about which ones are making you money, and which ones aren't', he says. Are you able to increase your prices? Should you shed some of your more troublesome customers and then redeploy your resources to areas of your business that can make you more money? All these strategies will have an impact on your bottom line. The trick is to be decisive, take action and communicate the importance of everyone in your team toeing the line. In *Manage for All Seasons*, Godbee tells the story of Sun Tzu, the master military strategist: 'If the general has told the troops what must be done and the troops do not understand, then the general is at fault. If the general then explains it well and checks that it is understood and the troops still do not comply, then the troops are at fault. And heads must roll. If it sounds harsh to lay off 20 per cent of your workforce when necessary, remember that the receiver will lay off 100 per cent soon if you do not act now'.

Action item: profit calculator

Some cost control and change management scenarios affect your business's bottom line more quickly than others. The Tasmanian Government's Department of Economic Development, Tourism and the Arts offers an online tool called a Profit Growth Calculator to help you decide what will give you the biggest impact in tough times. Go to <www.development.tas. gov.au>, click on 'Business in Tasmania', then 'Business Tools and Templates' and punch your own numbers into the spreadsheet.

Healthy businesses

Strong leaders know 'that it's six times more profitable to sell to an existing customer than to find new ones', suggests Kathryn Conder, partner of executive and business mentoring firm Carnegie Management Group. Fostering relationships and giving great customer service are imperative: it's your customers, clients and suppliers who will sustain you through tough times.

'Take the example of a cafe owner I know', she says. 'They had a couple who were regular customers: they would come in for breakfast every Sunday, sitting at their usual (reserved) favourite table. That customer was worth about $1500 to $2000 a year to the business. One Mother's Day, the customers walked in and the cafe was full. They were told there was no room for them, so they walked out and haven't been back since.'

Another consideration is what your team thinks about the state of play. 'Get them engaged and thinking about how you can all do this better', says Conder. After all, five people working out a better way to do your business is better than one. 'People who are motivated and interested and who enjoy coming to work each day are a key indicator of a healthy business', she adds.

Successful turnarounds

Graham Godbee lists five key factors you need for a successful business turnaround: know what is happening; know what to do; be decisive; push it through; and have enough time. For this you need good analysis and strong leadership. 'Determine whether urgent survival action is required or if you have time for a more considered business improvement program', he writes. Don't waste any time you have. Set yourself some realistic short-term goals: they will give you and your team something to work towards. This sort of planning will also help you feel in control of your destiny.

There are no hard and fast rules, and it does depend on what the sales cycle looks like in your business, says Kathryn Conder. 'If you had a bad six months that's gone to 12 months, or 12 months to two years, you might think, "Enough!"' The key is to give your business an honest appraisal: is 80 per cent of what you're doing going well and only 20 per cent not going so well? Or is it the other way around? If it's the other way, adopt a triage strategy for the part of your business that's bleeding. And ask for outside help from advisers you trust, such as your accountant or solicitor or other successful businesspeople you know.

Five ways to increase your profit

According to the Tasmanian Department of Economic Development, Tourism and the Arts, you can increase your profits by addressing one or more of the following five areas of your operations:

- Increase your exposure to current and potential buyers of your product or service.

- Increase your sales strike rate with new customers.

- Increase how often buyers come back to purchase from you.

- Increase how much people buy in a transaction.

- Decrease the costs needed to create your product or service or increase your prices.

Source: Tasmanian Department of Economic Development, Tourism and the Arts <www.development.tas.gov.au>.

Look in the mirror

Any business dramas should be able to be sorted out in a week or two ('At least 60 to 70 per cent of it', says Godbee). However, for this to happen you need to be honest with your own shortfalls. Conder agrees: 'Often the first place you need to look is in the mirror', she says. Is your management style part of the problem? If it is, you have the power to transform yourself. Spend time on your own development and learn more about the things you're not great at, whether it's cost control or people management or something else. What about some of your other business processes: are they in need of an overhaul too? If you're slow to pay your accounts, find out why and then speed up your system. If you're holding too much stock, maybe it's time for a sale. If your cash flow is tight, think about what you could do differently. There's simply no point, she says, believing that if you just work harder, it'll all be all right.

5 **Question:** *What are my options when it comes to structuring my business?*

Answer: *It pays to consider how your business structure will cope when you want to grow.*

The way you set up a business always seems like a good idea at the time. Often you start it on your own, so you opt for a sole trader status. You might have family in it with you, so you form a family trust. Or you go into a partnership with a friend. It works well in the short and medium term, but what about in terms of your future operations? Would a company structure now suit you better? Is it too late to change? No, says Kathryn Conder of Carnegie Management Group: 'While it's best to start as you intend to go on, when your business grows your business structure can be changed'.

First things first

To register or change your business structure, you'll need to contact the Australian Business Register (ABR) and advise it that you need a new Australian Business Number (ABN). You can do this online at <www.abr.gov.au>. Or you can phone the Australian Taxation Office (ATO) Business Infoline on 13 28 66, or contact your accountant or registered tax agent. Keeping the ATO abreast of your plans, and getting its advice, could save you some major hassles down the road. If you want to register, or change, any contact or ownership details for any patents, trademarks or designs you may have, you should contact IP Australia on 1300 651 010 or online at <www.ipaustralia.gov.au>.

Experts say that the most revised small business structures are sole traders, partnerships and trusts. Why? Because they seem to be the ones that start off with good intentions, but the purpose of the structure is often not thought through. Other business structures — proprietary limited companies, cooperatives and incorporated associations — tend to be changed less often because doing so costs you money (you can find more information on these structures and the costs involved in restructuring at the Australian Government's business advisory gateway <www.business.gov.au>). So let's focus on some of the pros and cons of common business structures.

Sole traders

A sole trader is exactly that: an individual trading on his or her own. You might have a business name, or be operating under your own name. You are the one responsible for all debts. Sole traders pay business income tax at personal tax rates. According to the ATO, low business profits in a sole trader structure may be taxed at rates below 30 per cent. High profits can be taxed above the company tax rate of 30 per cent. In terms of your liability, it's unlimited, which means that if something goes seriously wrong and you're sued, your personal assets can't be protected. This personal liability issue is one of the reasons to examine at your sole trader structure. You could consider a company structure for your business; however, because of the complex nature of company laws and obligations, you really need to investigate this with the help of your solicitor or accountant. The benefit of starting out as a sole trader is that you have all the other business structure options at your disposal when the time is right.

Partnerships

Partnerships are always set up with the best intentions. You have someone else along for the ride, sharing the costs, celebrating the successes and commiserating the losses. According to <www.business.gov.au>, partnerships are simple structures, both legally and financially. The downside is that all liabilities are unlimited, and partners are jointly liable for all debts incurred by the partnership (whether you were responsible for them or not). There are partnerships that thrive, with both partners dancing to the same beat. However, stories abound of partnerships that have turned to mush for myriad reasons. Maybe one partner wants things his way; or she wants out; or maybe your dream partner dies and you're left dealing with the fallout from the family.

The easy way to avoid a lot of the potential stress of partnerships is to draw up a partnership agreement. While it may not hold up legally if your partnership goes sour, it does tend to sort out the bones of your business, before they have to be picked over! You'll find a lot of advice on partnership agreements online (start at <www.business.gov.au>). Write down things such as the start date and duration of the partnership; who makes the decisions; exactly how property and any leases are to be handled; how profits, capital and losses are going to be distributed; and what happens if the partnership is dissolved or altered. To make any changes to a partnership agreement, or if you want to get out of the partnership structure altogether, it's wise to get the advice of a solicitor or an independent accountant.

Trusts

Has your operation grown so much that your original structure isn't cutting it when it comes to your tax requirements? One of the legal ways to minimise your tax obligations is to set up a trust. The ATO defines a trust as the responsibility of holding property or income for the benefit of others (known as the trust's beneficiaries). There are different types of trusts, and the costs to set them up vary (you can get some idea from the ATO website <www.ato.gov.au>). Every trust has to have its own tax file number, which is used to distribute funds to the trust's beneficiaries (the amount of tax and the distribution of funds process varies from trust to trust).

Action item: online information

There's some good, and free, business structure information that you can access online. Just don't make any decisions until you've spoken with an accountant who has experience in business structures, or your solicitor.

- ▫ The Australian Government's business portal <www.business.gov.au> has a number of sections relating to business structures (start by clicking on 'Registration & licences', then 'Decide on a business structure').

- ▫ The ATO has a *Tax basics for small business* booklet that's worth having a look at if you're not sure of the different tax liabilities for different business structures. You can access this from the ATO's website at <www.ato.gov.au> or phone 13 28 66 for a copy.

- ▫ If you're considering a company structure, you should first go to the Australian Securities & Investments Commission (ASIC) website <www.asic.gov.au> or call 1300 300 630.

The best idea if you're thinking about a trust structure, or any of the other business structures for that matter, is to do your research and talk to someone experienced in business structures (such as your accountant or solicitor). 'It really depends on your goals: where do you want your business to be in three, five and 10 years?' asks Conder. Look to your future and consider what's really going to work in your favour from a tax and liability point of view. Don't expect miracles to come from a particular business structure. But you can make it work in your favour.

6 **Question:** *What's the big deal about business plans when everyone seems to do well without them?*

Answer: *A business plan gets your vision out of your head so you have some tangible goals to aim for, and celebrate!*

Most people start their small businesses without a formal business plan. They have their vision for what they want to achieve in their heads, and some even boast about doing well without ever having put a plan down on paper. However, running your own business is no different to any other adventure in life. If you check a roadmap to make sure you know where you're going on holidays, and that it's the quickest route, why not do the same in your business? The majority of small businesses don't plan to fail, they just fail to plan. The humble piece of paper that is your business plan can help you, and your team, to work towards some tangible goals.

Reasons to have a plan

There are more reasons than that to have a business plan. Having a written plan prepares you for the day you need bank finance or investors to grow (see question 14 for tips on dealing with financiers). They will want to see a bit of strategic thinking before they will loan you money. They also like an outline of when they will get their investment back and how you will make this happen. Then there's the day you may want to exit your business (more on this in question 50). Even the keenest purchaser will want to know they're getting a good buy rather than a rotten egg. Having a written business plan could save you a lot of time and lost sleep if you ever decide to sell up.

Action item: planning tutorial

The Queensland Department of Employment, Economic Development and Innovation has an online *How to draw up a business plan* tutorial. Go to its site at <http://sd.qld.gov.au> and roll over 'Our Activities' and click on 'Business Development'. Click on the 'Starting a Business' checklist. Go to the 'Time to Plan' link, then the 'Smart Skills' link. Click on 'Business Planning' to start the free interactive tutorial. Why not take the five to 10 minutes to do it, particularly if you don't believe in business plans? You might be surprised what you learn!

Things to include

Much of the small business denial over business plans is in the perceived formality of it all. But it doesn't have to be a stitched-up thesis. It could be a document that simply lists your business goals, and how you think you'll achieve them. Think of the document as a set of instructions that could save you some serious frustrations along the way. It certainly doesn't have to be perfect. A one-page plan that covers your goals for the next 12 months of business is a good place to start. You can work up to putting down your three- to five-year goals later.

→ There are also some handy online templates you can use from federal, state and territory government websites (plus you can use the Business Plan appendix at the back of this book). The Queensland Department of Employment, Economic Development and Innovation also has a handy *How to Write a Business Plan* fact sheet on its website — see the breakout box above for details on how to get to the link. Then there's the Tasmanian Government's Department of Economic Development, Tourism and the Arts, which offers a free comprehensive PDF, Planning your Business Success, which includes

a business plan checklist (start at <www.development.
tas.gov.au>, then go to the 'Starting Your Business' link.
Scroll over the 'Planning Your Business' link, then click
on 'How do you create a business plan?', which takes you
to the PDF). Remember, it's not the actual paper itself but
the process of the plan (and the thinking behind it) that's
going to be beneficial to your business. In your business
plan, you could include your:

- *mission statement*. It's your reason for being.
  Having it at the beginning of your business plan
  allows you to bring everything in your plan back to
  this idea.

- *current situation*. Where your business is at now. This
  is where you put in facts from your SWOT (strengths,
  weaknesses, opportunities and threats) analysis (see
  breakout box, p. 25), any market trends and what
  your competition is up to.

- *plans*. What do you want to achieve in your business
  in the next 12 months? Write it down, and then add
  how you're going to get there. What sort of resources
  will you need? What about extra staff? How long will
  it take?

- *marketing*. Exactly who are you selling your wares to
  and how will you get your message to them? What
  about a website? Getting all your ideas down in black
  and white will give you some measurable goals to
  work towards.

- *operations*. This covers what you do and how you
  do it, from the purchasing of raw materials to
  any manufacturing or importing processes. It also
  includes who's involved and how you get the final
  product or service to the customer.

- *budget.* Listing your existing or expected income and expenditure gives you the playing field on which you operate. If you have plans to expand into other markets, does your budget support the plan? If it doesn't, what do you plan to do to make it happen?

- *evaluation.* Give yourself a timeline for review of the business plan, and some sort of way to gauge how things are going. Is it the bottom line, or whether what you've achieved is in line with your mission statement and marketing plan?

The 10-minute SWOT

A business plan will help you identify your strengths (S), weaknesses (W), opportunities (O) and threats (T). This is known as a SWOT analysis. It can help you do business with your eyes wide open, in good times and bad.

□ *Strengths.* Ask yourself what advantages you have over your competitors.

□ *Weaknesses.* Ask yourself what you could improve. Do these two things reveal any opportunities for your business?

□ *Opportunities.* Which areas offer the best chance of growth?

□ *Threats.* What are the obstacles you face, either within your business or from your competitors? Could you turn them into opportunities?

When a plan fails

There are two main reasons your business plan could come unstuck. Firstly, you may have written up a great one, but then you've simply filed it away and you don't give it a second thought. This tends to happen a lot when things are going well. Hit a speed hump, however, and you might have to adjust everything in your business, from your marketing and sales strategies to your workforce. That's why a business plan should be a living, breathing document that's constantly reviewed. For example, what will you do if your competitors drop their price: how low can you go? And if your manufacturing costs rise, what can you do to absorb them? By continually revising your business plan, you won't end up running around dodging the falling coconuts. You'll have planned for them before they fall out of the tree.

The other reason business plans fail is because you didn't get the buy-in of others in your business. Maybe you were the one to pull the business plan together, and your partners didn't really commit to what's been put down on paper. Or your staff have no idea what the plan is about because you haven't communicated it to them. For a plan to be effective, everyone has to be on the same page (literally) from the word go. And make sure everyone in the business contributes to some of the elements. If your business plan is something you all keep coming back to and developing as you go along, it will help you steer your ship.

Question: *Where do I look for advice and how much will it cost?*

Answer: *Start with recommendations from people you already trust.*

Small business owners can cop advice from every corner. Because you run your own show, you're fair game to friends, family and perfect strangers who are more than happy to give you their business tips, whether you ask for them or not. The hard part for you, when you're so immersed in your business, is to find the right kind of advice, on everything from your finances to marketing, at the right time, and the right price.

Finding good advisers

You want to be able to completely trust the professional advice you get from a range of experts. If you don't have good tax advice, for example, it could cost you thousands of dollars. Not covering your basic legal obligations could put you out of business. If you don't yet have good business advisers, or you'd like to change the ones you have, it's wise to ask friends and family for names of professionals they trust. If they can't give you any names, try asking some other local business owners for their recommendations.

Reputable advisers are usually members of their relevant professional association. It's worth contacting these associations directly as they can put you in touch with practitioners that you could trust with your business. The cost of professional advice varies from adviser to adviser, depending on their area and level of expertise. Always check an adviser's credentials and levels of professional indemnity insurance cover before you sign up.

Here is a list of some of the advisers that you might need in your business life:

→ *accountant*. A good accountant can give you standard finance, tax accounting and business advice. Ask your friends or family who they use (then check the referral out yourself). Best practice accountants are members of CPA Australia. To find a CPA accountant in your area, go to <www.cpaaustralia.com.au> and click on 'About CPA Australia' then 'Find a CPA' or call 1300 73 73 73.

→ *bookkeeper*. A thorough bookkeeper can save you time (preparing your BAS) and money (good ones will pick up any mistakes). The Australian Association of Professional Bookkeepers has a list of its members nationally at <www.aapb.org.au>.

→ *solicitor or lawyer*. Word-of-mouth referrals are best as your relationship with your business solicitor is all about trust and confidentiality. You can also contact the Law Society in your state or territory (do an online search or look it up in the *Yellow Pages*).

→ *insurance broker*. Brokers can find the best insurance for your business at the best price. Start your search by looking for brokers who are members of the National Insurance Brokers Association (NIBA). Go directly to its online national insurance broker locator at <www.needabroker.com.au>.

→ *business broker*. You might need a business broker if you decide to sell your business (see question 50), or acquire a new one. There are reams of them listed in the *Yellow Pages*; good ones are members of the Australian Institute of Business Brokers <www.aibb.org.au>.

→ *human resources consultants*. Most small business owners are their own human resources department. You manage, hire and fire staff. However, if your business is growing (you were a team of five, now you're 10, and you're looking to double your head count again in the future), it would be wise to enlist the services of an HR consultant. They are trained in setting up systems, policies and procedures to give your business some sort of structure and to make sure you're compliant with government workplace regulations (more on this in question 35). An HR consultant can also assist you with recruitment and help you train your team. Look for HR consultants that are members of the Australian Human Resources Institute <www.ahri.com.au>.

→ *marketing expert*. You know your product, but do you know how to get it noticed? A professional marketer might be worth a call. Prices, and the range of services they offer, vary. You'll find marketing experts listed in the *Yellow Pages*. Check their credentials: they should be members of a professional marketing assocation, such as

the Marketing Association of Australia and New Zealand
<www.marketing.org.au> or the Australian Marketing
Institute <www.ami.org.au>.

→ *website developer.* A good web developer can create a
site that gets your business noticed by customers even
while you're asleep (for the tricks of search engine
optimisation, see question 29). For experienced
developers, start your search at the Australian Web
Industry Association <www.webindustry.com.au>.

→ *graphic artist.* Packaging your product and designing
your logo is an important part of branding your
business. Get it right with the help of a good graphic
artist and you'll stand out in a crowded marketplace.
Check the Australian Graphic Design Association
database <www.agda.com.au> for designers who adhere
to the industry's code of ethics.

→ *IT expert.* When things go wrong with your office
technology, they usually go really wrong. Keep the local
IT or computer expert's phone number where everyone
in your office can see it. If you haven't engaged anyone's
services to date, ask other businesses who they use or
look in the *Yellow Pages*.

Before you pay for any advice, it's worth brushing up on
business jargon so you won't be bamboozled by adviser-
speak. Knowing what you need and preparing some of the
information before you see an adviser will also save you
time in front of them, and this will save you money. There
are lots of federal, state and territory government department
websites that can help you decipher business terms (some
even have checklists to fill out before you seek professional
help). Start with the Australian Government's business portal
<www.business.gov.au>, the Queensland Department of
Tourism, Regional Development and Industry's Smart Skills
site <www.business.qld.gov.au> and the national network of
not-for-profit Business Enterprise Centres <www.beca.org.au>.

Action item: caution

Talk to at least two business consultants, accountants or lawyers before you sign up an adviser's services. Avoid any adviser who:

- tries to sell you products at the first meeting

- isn't listening to you and your goals

- promises great returns or tries to sell you 'get rich quick' schemes — this is bad advice

- displays body language that is not consistent with what they are saying.

Attributed to Business Victoria <www.businessvictoria.vic.gov.au>.

What to ask an adviser

When you do track down an adviser you like the look of, ask him or her to give you a couple of names of people he or she has helped in the past. Suss out these referrals before you make a commitment. And find out exactly how much every bit of business advice will cost you. When you meet the adviser for the first time, go armed with a list of questions. Does the adviser listen to you? Are your questions answered? Do you feel comfortable with the communication? In the future your adviser might get pretty up close and personal with your business details, so the relationship needs to be working well from the start.

Good advice can transform your business, or take it to the next level. But to make it work, you have to be clear from the word go about your expectations. Know the outcomes you want, and the time frame you want these to happen in. Then commit the time to find the best adviser you can. It's worth the effort.

8

Question: *Why do my clients think I'm the only one they can call?*

Answer: *Nurturing them into a new relationship with your trusted team will free you up.*

Clients *do* get a kick out of calling you, even when your business grows. You're the one they've always called. You're the one they think of when they have a question about your product or service. We've all seen successful people taking phone calls on holidays, even in the middle of the golf course. But surely this should only happen in extreme circumstances: in an emergency? The trouble is, as a small business owner it's easy to become so entwined in the day-to-day operation of your business that you can't give it up. Maybe you don't want to. However, if you can't let go of things in your down time, you'll have no down time at all.

Forward thinking

Doing the big deals yourself might still pay off. But how many other deals are you missing out on because you don't have the time to develop other markets? Sure, your business might grow naturally, but shouldn't you be working on new opportunities? Is fielding all the calls from current customers making the best use of your skills, and your time? Who's directing the future business strategy of your enterprise?

'Unless you change, you may do the business more harm than good', says Associate Professor Isabel Metz, an expert in organisational behaviour at Melbourne Business School. The change, she says, is all in your mindset: start behaving more like a 'participative leader'. This is someone who lets go and empowers the team to do the business and make their own decisions. Research shows this is critical for business owners. The hard part for you, however, could be in the letting go.

It's all about trust

You had the great idea for your business. And you've been brilliant at the exchanges with your customers. But now it's time to include others in your plans so that you can have a life, or at least plan for the next stage of your business growth. It means thinking about your team, and who you'd trust to nurture the relationships you've created with your customers. You then have to trust that they can do it. 'By surrounding yourself with capable people you trust, you should be able to do this', says Metz. Developing your people is paramount (see more on this in question 21). Empowering them with your standards of excellence is critical.

Keeping your customers happy

Whether you're a small or big business, the principles of creating a customer service culture are the same, according to the NSW Department of Fair Trading. In a report entitled *How happier customers can lead to healthier business*, the department suggests managing your service culture by:

- creating a customer service environment across your whole business that is specifically aligned with your customers' needs and focuses on customer retention

- having and actively following a customer service charter which clearly sets out the quality of service your customers can expect from you

- ensuring that your business's policies, practices, systems, rules, facilities and staff actively provide for excellent customer service delivery

- integrating your customer service strategy into your overall approach and plans

- □ creating a structure and culture that enables high levels of staff satisfaction, and rewards staff for their ability to deliver excellent customer service

- □ ensuring you have mechanisms in place to obtain regular, reliable feedback from your customers about their needs and your service

- □ actively encouraging quality service and continuous improvement in everything your business does. This requires ongoing examination of underlying causes which create or tolerate service problems, and changes in practices which created the problems

- □ ensuring your business always complies with the fair trading laws as a natural complement to best practice customer service.

Source: NSW Department of Fair Trading <www.consumer.gov.au/html/pdf/servicebook.pdf>.

The handover

Relationships and trust are built over time, but there's no time like today to plan how you're going to hand over the day-to-day communication with customers. When you have your next meeting with your client, take your employee along. Show the client that you value this staffer's opinion. Drop into the conversation how well this person handled another customer's problem. Allow your employee to give the client a glimpse of his or her knowledge, experience and expertise. In this way, the employee is enhancing his or her credibility. You're showing that you trust your employee, so maybe your client should too.

At this stage you can even include your staff member in any socialising with the customer so this person can start building relationships. Instil the philosophy that the customer mightn't always be right, but they're always the customer. If there's a hiccup in the relationship during the handover period, the worst thing you can do is step in. Your employee's credibility will be shot. And your clients will continue to call you, long after they should be calling someone else on your team.

Steady as she goes

Sometimes a handover can happen quickly, but only if your client's happy. If they haven't been told that you want to start empowering your team to take their calls, they might feel like they're simply being dumped by you. This is the last thing you want to happen. As in any relationship, being dumped is disastrous. So easy does it. 'There should be a feeling of transition during which you all work together', says Metz. The length of this transition will depend on your business, and your customers. Just make sure you give customers time to feel like they're making their own decision about the new relationship. Initially, give them the option of still being able to call you, but let them know that they can trust your staff member, because you do.

Rethink your role

It's fine in theory to hand over the client contact to a member of your team. But then you can be left feeling as though you've lost control. Get over it. You're the main cog in this machine. Sure, you're stepping out of the daily monitoring, the daily control. However, you'll actually be more in control of your whole business, creating a culture of good performance and good service. Isn't this the sort of thing you'd pay money for?

Reflect for a second on your vision for the business: if you set it up to eventually give you more freedom, start planning for it. At some point in your business development, whether it's now or a year down the track, you're going to have to start trusting that others can do just as good a job as you have in lots of areas of your business. Make the time to guide your employees into great relationships with your customers. Then you'll have time to concentrate on the bigger picture. And think of those family and friend moments, weekends and holidays that will no longer be interrupted by a client call. That's surely worth the effort.

Part II

Business, BAS and banks

In this part, you'll find the answers to many of your finance-, tax- and accounting-based questions. There's expert advice on managing your cash flow, and tips on myriad other financial machinations, from unravelling your tax requirements to deciding how much debt you should take on. All of these things are often the bane of small business owners, but they don't have to be.

Some of the issues covered here, such as cash flow, cost and credit queries, have whole books written about them. So you should always go to see your accountant or business adviser for advice that's going to be right for your specific business.

9

Question: *Is there a way to make my accounts easier?*

Answer: *Understanding accounting–speak is a good start.*

Your accounts are the pulse monitor of your business. 'If you cannot measure it, you cannot manage it', says Dr Graham Godbee of the Macquarie Graduate School of Management, in his book *Manage for All Seasons* (which you can download for free by clicking on the 'Resources' section of the Terris Business Consultants site <www.terris.com.au>). Knowing what your accounts mean and how to check them are two of the most important skills you can have under your belt. If your business's pulse is strong and all's going well, you can keep concentrating on the things that inspire you, such as growing your business. If the pulse is racing or too slow, you'll know enough about what this really means and what to do to be able to get it back to a normal beat.

Where to start

There are different ways of looking at your business from an accounting point of view. And mountains of accounting jargon in the way. Here's some of the lingo you'll do well to understand:

→ *Accrual accounting.* This is when you put your revenues alongside your expenses over a particular time frame. The aim, according to Godbee, is to provide 'a "true" measure of how well the organisation has performed in the period (that is, what was its true profit)'. The building blocks of accrual accounting are the balance sheet ('what we own and what we owe') and the income statement ('what we sold and what it cost us').

→ *Cash accounting.* This is simply when cash comes in and out of a business from your sales and expenses.

Says Godbee: 'There is no consideration about assets or liabilities and therefore no balance sheet'. What it does give you is an indication of your cash flow. Even profitable companies (that look positive on the balance sheet and income statement) can go bust if they don't have enough cash flow to sustain the business (see more on this in question 10).

Which is better?

Godbee thinks that cash accounting doesn't give a true picture of a business. What if you have done all the work, incurred expenses and sold some of your goods and services, he asks, but the customer won't be paying until the next accounting period? 'Under cash accounting for this period, we will have all the expenses and none of the revenue so we will show a loss. Such a loss would infer poor performance but we have actually performed well to make the goods efficiently and make a sale.' Using the accrual accounting method, however, you account for the sale when the goods or services have been delivered, regardless of when the customer pays you. 'The outstanding payment would be recorded as an asset of accounts receivable in the balance sheet', says Godbee. Any capital expenses, such as major equipment or machinery, are noted as an asset, and their value (which gets eroded from their purchase price each year) would be recorded as an expense against that year's revenue. This expense is called depreciation.

Are professional bookkeepers worth the money?

It can be worth employing the services of a qualified book-keeper to get your books in good shape. Then it's easier for you to manage them. 'You need to figure whether you as the business owner can get more value by spending your time in the business or doing the books', says regional director of H&R Block <www.hrblock.com.au>

Frank Brass. You can pay anything from $20 to $70 per hour for a bookkeeper. If he or she is an authorised BAS Service Provider with the ATO, you may be charged more. Get referrals from other small businesses or ask your accountant for a recommendation. Remember, while a good bookkeeper can organise your accounts and save you time, the buck ultimately stops with you. So always cast your eye over what has been done.

Reading a balance sheet

Godbee says you can think of the balance sheet as the two sides of your business. One side has assets which you own. The other side has liabilities and owners' equity, which you owe other people.

On the assets side of the balance sheet you have:

→ *current assets* (you expect to convert these into cash in the next 12 months). These include cash, accounts receivable, inventory (stock) and prepayments

→ *non-current (or fixed) assets* (they won't be converted into cash in the next 12 months). These include buildings and land owned by the business, plant and equipment, office equipment and motor vehicles, plus other assets such as investments and goodwill.

On the liabilities side of the balance sheet you have:

→ *current liabilities* (you will have to pay for these in the next 12 months). Included here are bank loans, business credit cards and overdrafts, accounts payable to creditors, income and PAYG tax payable, GST liabilities and other accrued expenses

→ *non-current liabilities* (they don't need to be paid in the next 12 months). These include mortgages, lease payments and provisions for employee entitlements.

Getting the most out of accounting packages

Keeping accurate records is a legal requirement of you as a small business owner. There are many different acc-ounting software packages that claim to make your life easier by doing all your accrual accounting calculations and generating easy-to-read reports. The most popular commercial products are MYOB and QuickBooks. However, if your business's financial structure is fairly simple (that is, you use cash accounting methods, have paper records such as ledger books and one bank account), the Australian Taxation Office has a free online tool called e-Record that can reconcile sales records and bank statements, and help you complete your BAS statement (for more on BAS and your tax liabilities, see question 11). Check it out at <www.ato.gov.au/nonprofit/content.asp?doc=/content/61182.htm>.

To get the most (in the shortest possible time) out of any brand of accounting software, H&R Block's Frank Brass suggests you sign up for a user course so that you under-stand the types of information it's capable of giving you, before you need it. He also recommends you get all your data entered into the system regularly: don't leave it until your BAS is due. If you need to hire a bookkeeper to do this for you to save you time, do it.

Reading an income statement

Godbee points out that the income statement is basically a summary of your business transactions for a set period (say, a year) that lead to a profit or loss for the business. The transactions are labelled under revenue (including sales, fees earned, rent and interest earned) and expenses (such as wages, interest, cost of goods and advertising). Your revenues minus your expenses is your profit (or loss). However, he adds that numbers aren't always what they seem: 'With accrual accounting, recognition of revenues and expenses does not necessarily match up in time with cash flows'.

Keeping it all in balance

There are some simple things you can do when it comes to your admin so that you'll always know how healthy your business is:

→ *Do daily backups of data.* You don't ever want to lose your daily sales and expenses information. Download it on a separate backup system.

→ *Do your filing.* Getting your paperwork organised the moment it comes in will save you a lot of frustration.

→ *Schedule time to do the books.* If you don't make the time to go through things, how will you know what your cash flow's looking like?

→ *Automate important payments.* Just make sure you have money in the bank to cover them.

→ *Stick to your payment terms.* Again, it helps you manage your cash flow, and it really is good business.

→ *Do your BAS on time.* You're obliged to do it, and you'll be on the Tax Office radar if you don't (see more on your BAS in question 11).

→ *Review reports regularly.* Use the data to review your business plan every six months.

→ *Keep your accounting software up to date.* Install all updates and pay for the latest versions of software as the systems are being improved all the time.

→ *Reconcile your bank accounts every month.* That way you will always know your cash position.

→ *Chase your debtors.* Don't let suppliers draw out their credit terms. Stay on their case (for more on debt recovery, see question 41).

→ *Reconcile your loans and any money you owe to suppliers.* By doing this every month your business won't ever fly blind.

10 Question: *Why is cash flow my biggest stress?*

Answer: *Because if there's no cash, you literally don't have a business.*

Cash flow is the amount of money that comes in and goes out of your business. The stress comes from the fact that if there's no cash, you can't pay your debts. And if you can't pay your debts, you don't have a business. However, according to a 2007 survey by the Australian Bureau of Statistics, called *Selected Characteristics of Australian Business,* 14 per cent of businesses reported not focusing on financial measures at all, and 18 per cent of businesses reported not focusing on cost measures when assessing their business performance. It was an even worse result for micro businesses (with none to four persons employed): 18 per cent reported not focusing on financial measures; and 23 per cent didn't focus on cost measures. Sure, working out how your business is performing financially takes time. But experts agree that if you don't work out your current and future cash flows, your business is flying blind.

Why is cash flow vital?

Even profitable businesses can go bust if their cash flow is seriously out. Often it's all about timing. If you're not going to have enough cash to pay your bills this month, how can you prove to a bank that it will be all okay next month? They're going to want some answers, particularly if you've asked them for an overdraft to get through a shortfall in cash (see more on this in question 16). How long will you need this cash injection for? And if you don't know your cash position, how would you know whether or not you can afford to give your customers credit?

Grasping the basics of cash flow can help you lay out your options for times when cash is tight. The first thing to understand is that cash flow is different to profit. 'Profit is about measuring performance', says Dr Graham Godbee of the Macquarie Graduate School of Management and author of *Manage for All Seasons*. 'Cash flow tells us about viability.' If your cash flow from operations (the amount of revenue coming in minus paying out for purchases, wages, rent and so on) is negative and you don't have the cash to pay your bills on time, your business is in trouble.

Working it out

Graham Godbee thinks the best way to protect your business from crashing without cash is to do a cash flow forecast. Simply calculate how much cash — petty cash and cash in the bank — your business has access to. 'You can include some cash equivalents like short-term bank bills you own (not borrowings) and maybe some publicly listed shares that can be readily liquidated', he says. Write it all down. Then look at how much cash it takes to keep your business operating on a daily or weekly basis. You should always keep in mind that your analysis can vary from week to week, depending on when major cash flows (both in and out) are expected in your business. Godbee tells the story of a firm that pays its workers each fortnight. It should make its cash flow periods two weeks apart: 'If it uses monthly periods, it may find it does not have the cash to pay wages one pay day in the middle of the month'.

Action item: cash flow forecast template

Some Australian state and territory governments have cash flow forecast templates on their business development websites. Have a look to get you started. The Northern Territory Government offers an easy-to-use template at <www.nt.gov.au/business/documents/general/CASH_FLOW_FORECAST.pdf>.

What to include

Work out what you need to spend on things such as wages, rent, consumables and utilities. 'This is sometimes given the fancy term "cash burn rate" by finance people', says Godbee. The cash burn rate is simple if you think of it in terms of how much cash it would take to keep your business operating if no new cash comes in. 'For example, you have $60 000 on hand (in the bank and in the safe). Your business goes through about $5000 of cash per week. So $60 000 ÷ $5000 = 12 weeks of operations until the cash is gone.' He says if you know how much cash will be coming in to your business, you can adjust the calculation: 'If, for example, you can be reasonably confident that $2000 will come in each week, then the net cash burn rate will drop to $3000 per week. In this case, there is then 20 weeks of cash available for operations'.

Finding out your cash burn rate gives you a general idea of how your cash flow is holding up right now. However, business doesn't just exist in the now; you also want it to be about the future. That's why Godbee advises businesses to invest time in a more in-depth cash flow forecast, and review it regularly. 'Ask yourself some basic questions about your future: what if you increase your sales; what if customers delay payments; what if you expand and buy some new equipment; what if costs rise; what if sales or prices fall; and so on.'

As well as looking at how much cash is in your bank account, look at things such as the investments and assets that you could easily liquidate if you had to, and how much is left in unused lines of credit. 'Are additional borrowings possible and sensible?' he asks. 'Is there scope for additional equity injections immediately? Is there immediate expenditure that can be cancelled or deferred (for example, capital expenditure)? Can you stall creditor payments legally?'

It might take you a fair few hours to find out the answers to these questions, but in the end you'll be able to put together an accurate cash flow forecast. Doing this can only help your business go from strength to strength. It also will take a lot of the operational stress out of your day. Godbee adds: 'If you want to stay in business, if you want to impress your bank manager and if you want to keep your personal assets, then do your cash flow forecast!'

Warning signs of insolvency

A company becomes insolvent when it can't pay its debts on time (including wages and supplies). If you're the owner and you've allowed your company to continue trading while insolvent, your personal assets may be used to pay out the creditors. Imagine losing your house just because you couldn't be bothered doing a cash flow forecast! According to the Australian Securities & Investments Commission (ASIC), the signs of insolvency are:

- ongoing losses
- poor cash flow
- absence of a business plan
- delaying creditors well past normal terms
- dishonoured cheques (or post dating them)

Warning signs of insolvency *(cont'd)*

▫   overdrawn loan facilities

▫   special arrangements with some creditors.

Source: The Australian Securities & Investments Commission. For more information go to <www.asic.gov.au/insolvencyinfosheets>.

11   Question: *Should my BAS be such hard work?*

Answer: *Your regular admin systems might be letting you down.*

Every quarter it's the same: a mad scramble to get your BAS completed and your GST liabilities in to the Australian Taxation Office by the set deadline. Many small business owners get worked up over their BAS because of the deadlines and the fact that they've left it to the last minute, says Frank Brass, regional director of the national tax accountant firm H&R Block <www.hrblock.com.au>. Don't be one of them.

Your obligations

The best way to suss out all your tax responsibilities is to spend time going through the ATO website <www.ato.gov.au>. It has a heap of information (enough to fill a whole book on its own) regarding your tax obligations, including how to accurately fill in your BAS. Here are a few of the main points you need to know.

Goods and services tax

If you're an Australian business with an annual turnover (gross business income) of $75 000 or more you must register for GST (if you're a taxi or limousine business, you need to register regardless of your turnover). You can register for GST at the same time you apply for your ABN. Go to <www.business.gov.au> to do this. Once you're registered, you use a Business Activity Statement (which you're sent when you register, or you can do it all online) to report on your business's tax obligations (what you're collecting) and entitlements (what you've paid out). The one form includes GST (which is calculated by dividing the price of any good or service by 11. For example the GST on $100 is $9.09), PAYG instalments, PAYG withholding and FBT instalments (see below). There's a total to indicate your net liabilities once the obligations and entitlements are accounted for. You fill out a Business Activity Statement (BAS), and pay any liabilities, on a weekly, quarterly or annual basis (the ATO says most businesses do it quarterly).

To calculate your GST liability, you can use your own business accounting records, as long as you have 'separately recorded the GST amounts for your sales and purchases: for small businesses this may be as simple as having a GST column in your cashbook or spreadsheet,' states the ATO. You also will need tax receipts to prove you bought anything valued at over $50, excluding GST.

PAYG income tax instalments

Pay as you go (PAYG) instalments allow you to make down-payments towards your end-of-year income tax liability. The ATO says there are two PAYG payment options: instalment amounts (which are calculated by the ATO based on your annual income tax return) and the instalment rate (the ATO gives you a rate that you then multiply against your actual income). You write all your PAYG commitments on your BAS. The ATO advises that it's best to finalise your PAYG instalments before you lodge your annual income tax return so that they can help you work out exactly what you need to pay, and if you're entitled to a refund.

PAYG tax withheld

These are the PAYG tax amounts that you must withhold from your employees, contractors, company directors if you have them, or other businesses that don't give you their ABN on invoices. The ATO website has a whole slather of advice on when you should withhold PAYG tax, and stipulates that you should send all withheld amounts to the Tax Office with your activity statement (for details go to <www.ato.gov.au/businesses>, click on 'Lodge a business activity statement (BAS)/Activity statement essentials', then click on 'PAYG tax withheld/Overview').

Action item: keeping track of tax

The ATO offers small business owners a number of useful tools to help you keep track of all your tax obligations (you can access them all through <www.ato.gov.au>).

- There's a free electronic recordkeeping package (e-Record) to help you maintain accurate records and stay up to date with your tax obligations.

- The Small Business Assistance Program offers practical advice (a tax officer may even be able to come to your workplace) on everything from recordkeeping to filling out your BAS. Go to the 'Free help for small business' section of the ATO website.

- If you find you're running late with a GST payment, there's an online calculator to help you work out some payment scenarios and get you back on track.

Fringe benefits tax

You're obliged to pay fringe benefits tax (FBT) if you give your employees or their families benefits above and beyond their salary and wages. 'Examples of benefits include a car, car parking, low interest loan and payments of private expenses', states the Australian Government's business portal <www.business.gov.au>. If your FBT obligation for last year was $3000 or more, the ATO advises that you need to pay the tax by quarterly instalments with your BAS.

Meeting the deadline

The penalty for not completing your BAS on time is called the general interest charge (GIC). The rate of this charge changes every quarter (fluctuating between about 10 and 15 per cent of the amount you owe). You can find the current rate on the ATO's website.

Correcting any mistakes

The ATO encourages you to contact it the moment you know you've made an error that could impact your BAS. The worst thing you can do is do nothing. 'In some cases you can correct the mistake or omission in the GST section on a later activity statement', states the ATO. Correcting a mistake on a BAS is different from making an adjustment: an adjustment is made when prices for sales or purchases are different to your calculation; you make a correction if you've entered incorrect figures or left off amounts on your BAS.

Getting your systems sorted

The best way to minimise your BAS burden is to look at the admin systems you have in place. Simplify the way you collect your GST data. Frank Brass suggests you:

→ do your bookkeeping regularly so that when it comes around to BAS time, it's easy to wrap up

→ have columns indicating your GST ins and outs if you're still using handwritten ledger books to keep track of your accounts. This will make it easier to see the totals

→ enter accurate data into any accounting software on your computer, such as MYOB or QuickBooks (see more on these packages in question 9)

→ do a training course so that you have an idea of what goes into your business's books (even if you don't do them yourself). Even innocent mistakes can be costly.

Getting help

It's not in the Tax Office's interest to see your business get into tax trouble (it does like to be able to collect tax from you). It even says it is happy to consider payment extensions and pauses and fast-tracking GST refunds for small businesses. You just have to contact it and prove that your problems are legitimate. The ATO also has a *GST for Small Business Guide* (it's available in soft or hard copy at <www.ato.gov.au/business>, click on 'Tax Topics A-Z', 'F-G'/'Goods and Services Tax (GST)', then 'GST for small business') that's worth a look. And if you have any major queries about your BAS or GST obligations, always contact your accountant.

New developments

Every now and again the Tax Office does respond to economic conditions by changing some of its require-ments. For example, at the time of writing the ATO had created the Twelve-month General Interest Charge (GIC) Free payment arrangements. If you had an annual turnover of less than $2 million and an activity statement debt you could apply for help with your GIC payment. The ATO also started a credit card pilot in 2009. To keep up with any new developments that might ease your tax load, it's a good idea to visit the ATO website at least a couple of times a year (go on, add <www.ato.gov.au> to your Favourites).

12 Question: *Am I the only one worried about a tax audit?*

Answer: *Tax audits happen every day. Be honest and organised and you'll have nothing to worry about.*

Honest and reasonable. They're two words that Australian Taxation Office auditors carry around like badges of honour. If you run your business honestly, and do your best to have accurate records, you're considered to be doing a good job by the Tax Office. They're even happy to help you do a better one (see question 11). So there's really no need to worry about tax audits. Is there? In the 2007–08 financial year the ATO reported that 30 000 reviews and audits were conducted on GST liabilities alone. When it came to employers' compliance with their PAYG withholding, superannuation guarantee and FBT obligations, the ATO states that it carried out '290 field audits, 140 outbound telephone reviews and 6700 desk reviews'. The reality is that many Australian small businesses are being checked out every day.

The ATO says it's more intent on catching businesses with 'a reckless disregard' for the tax rules than chasing you for any bits you've missed from your books. If you make an honest attempt to comply with the complex tax laws, it states that it won't penalise you for an honest error (you may have to pay the GIC charge on the tax you haven't paid, but penalties will not apply). You can take control by getting your business records in great shape. That way, you shouldn't have anything to worry about.

Audit awareness

A lot of the panic about a potential tax audit is in the fear of the unknown, says Frank Brass of H&R Block. However, the ATO doesn't hide anything about the audit process: you can find out all you need to know on the ATO website

<www.ato.gov.au> or by calling it on its Business Infoline (13 28 66). According to the Tax Office, an audit or tax enquiry 'is an examination of your tax affairs … to see if you have done what you are required to do under the tax laws, including whether you: have declared all the assessable income you receive; and are entitled to the deductions and tax offsets you have claimed on your tax return'. The assumption is always that you've done your reasonable best to do the right thing.

Audits can be big or small; however, they're rarely sprung on you. (A tax officer will only arrive at your office unannounced if the ATO suspects you might destroy records they want to see.) First, you're sent a 'please explain' letter telling you the ATO has spotted that there might be an error in your tax return. Or you might get a phone call or another letter asking you for more information or to substantiate one of your claims with copies of receipts. Sometimes it'll then send out a field officer to visit your office; in other cases you're told to bring any relevant documentation in to the ATO, meaning it wants to see everything that justifies your tax return or BAS.

How you're chosen

There's usually method in its investigations. 'We sometimes decide to look more closely at tax returns making similar claims or from within the same industry', offers the ATO. The Tax Office can get information from various sources, including Centrelink and banks (which have to disclose any interest from your accounts). All it then has to do is check that everything matches up.

Depending on your industry, the ATO has benchmarks that it automatically compares your returns against. Frank Brass says that if your business is outside any of these benchmarks and business norms (including your economic performance), you could be targeted for an audit or a review. Sometimes it might get a tip-off from third parties, particularly when it comes to small businesses that operate in the cash economy. It also tends to target small businesses in their growth or exit phases.

What to expect

The ATO usually first does a 'review' of your books, which is less formal than an audit. In this process it will actually help you fix up any honest and reasonable mistakes. If it finds anything it wants to have a closer look at, it will formally request an audit. When this happens you're expected to give a tax officer 'full and free access to buildings, premises, records and documents'. You don't have to show them any documents from your solicitor or accountant as these are deemed professionally confidential. You are expected to let them photocopy any records and documents as well as help them conduct the audit comfortably by giving them a desk to sit at. You should be truthful and honest and 'provide complete, accurate and timely responses to requests for information', says the ATO.

The penalties

If a tax officer checks your records and discovers that your tax liability is out (understated) or you've tried to claim deductions to which you are not entitled, you'll be asked to pay back the outstanding amount. They warn that this could include interest. The degree of interest will depend on the reasons for the discrepancy. Any serious or repeated breaches of the tax laws could see you summonsed to court. 'These breaches include making false or misleading statements, failing to lodge returns or statements, and keeping incorrect or false records with an intention to deceive or mislead a tax officer', says the ATO. The fines for these offences range from $2000 to $10 000 plus a prison sentence of two years. The best idea is to stay on the straight and narrow when it comes to keeping correct records and you'll save yourself a lot of money and angst.

Protect yourself

You can insure yourself against some of the costs you might incur if you are going to be audited by the Tax Office. These costs include any fees you have to pay bookkeepers or accountants, or overtime you have to pay staff, to help you prepare for the audit. If you have to travel in to an ATO office, your travel expenses also could be covered by audit insurance. Most insurance companies can offer you audit insurance; just be certain you know exactly what it covers and if it also covers you for a less formal Tax Office review. And be aware that audit insurance won't cover you for any penalties that are imposed if the ATO finds you haven't fulfilled your tax obligations. That's up to you.

Action item: your tax audit checklist

A tax audit is a serious business. It really does pay to be prepared.

- *Keep good records.* The ATO admits it focuses on small businesses that it thinks haven't taken 'reasonable care' with their recordkeeping systems. So do it right in the first place. H&R Block's Frank Brass suggests you balance each period of your BAS to your books to make sure your tax returns agree with your BAS total for the year. (For more recordkeeping tips, see question 9.)

- *Be honest.* 'If it is an honest error, the ATO can be compassionate', says Brass. If you've been notified of an audit and you know there are mistakes in your books, get on the phone to the ATO and tell them about the discrepancies, before they come out to you.

- *Know the norms.* The Tax Office offers some benchmarks of what's acceptable when it comes to tax in your industry sector: 'Make sure your business is within the norms', says Brass.

- *Be prepared.* If you use an accountant or tax agent, let him or her know you're going to be audited and 'go through the records the Tax Office is requesting (including tax returns and activity statements) to make sure everything is there', Brass suggests. Also ask your accountant or someone you trust to be there during an on-site tax audit, although you're the one who will have to answer any questions.

- *Check credentials.* From a legal point of view, Peter Foster-Bunch of Legal Access Services <www.legalaccess.com.au> advises you to check an auditor's ID (they should also be carrying their tax audit authority) and 'ensure that the Commissioner or the approved delegate has signed the authority'.

- *Find room.* Although you have to allow an ATO officer 'full and free access', Foster-Bunch says this doesn't mean he or she has to have free rein around your office. You should also do any photocopying of original documents yourself so you know they've been copied correctly.

- *Record the audit.* Keep a record of everything that occurs during the audit, including the questions you're asked, your answers and every document you photocopy for the tax officer, advises Foster-Bunch. It'll help you remember the information you've given the auditor if you ever need it down the track.

13 **Question:** *How can I keep a lid on all of my business expenses?*

Answer: *Creating a cost management culture will help.*

In good times, your business expenses can often fly under the radar. There are lots of sales and stacks of profit so life is good. Staff spend up on travel, they order couriers to pick things up in an hour and deal with the suppliers they've always dealt with. But get to a downturn in business, and suddenly your cash flow isn't looking that flash. You quickly work out that you need to cut costs. But where?

Small expenses count

Print out your income statement (if you don't know what it is, quickly turn back to question 9) and have a look at where you and your staff are spending your money. According to Avron Newstadt, principal consultant with Expense Reduction Analysts, businesses often look at slashing large expenses, such as headcount and marketing, when times get tight. But it's the costs associated with telecommunications, insurance, recruitment, print, freight, travel and many other indirect costs that add up. 'As a result, many companies may be significantly overpaying on their products and services', he says. In his experience, overspending in these areas averages 20 per cent. But it doesn't have to be like this. For a start, he says you can ask your team to test the market when it comes to freight and couriers, telecommunications, energy, print and travel. 'If they can identify another supplier or renegotiate lower prices with existing suppliers of these services without reducing the quality of service or products, give them a reward.'

Dr Graham Godbee of the Macquarie Graduate School of Management says there are many unproductive expenses that you should always be ready to look at. In his book *Manage for All Seasons* he cites one example of a tyre dealer in the southern suburbs of Sydney. 'A quick analysis showed an unusually high expenditure on advertising in the St George Hospital magazine. The advertising as a percentage of sales was more than the net profit. When asked how many customers were brought in by the advertising, there was no idea (we suspect none). When we asked "why so much expenditure in this magazine", the answer was eventually elicited that the sales representative was a very attractive lady who would take the manager of the tyre business out to lunch regularly. We doubled the profits and lost no sales by cancelling this advertising. The manager also had less attractive lunches.'

Reigning them in

Never take your eye off your costs. That's the secret to creating a buoyant business, says Newstadt. He also suggests creating a cost culture, so that everyone you employ is motivated to keep their eyes on their expenses, too. 'This can be something as simple as asking all your staff to look outside the square for areas they can cut costs by 5 or 10 per cent', he says. Make sure they always understand what they are buying, and why. If an employee has a strong relationship with a supplier, get him or her to really identify if you're being charged market rate or the same rate you've paid since you first started your business. On <www.business.gov.au> the Australian Government suggests that looking at all these areas of your business is vital. Do plenty of research before anything major is bought for your business, and get quotes from more than one supplier, making sure suppliers are quoting on a like-for-like basis.

> **Action item: the small expenses count**
>
> For a cost-saving culture to work, you and your staff need to be aware of everything that's spent. Don't let the small expenses be the slow dripping tap that ends up costing your business more than it should over the

Action item *(cont'd)*: the small expenses count

course of the year. As an exercise, add up the following business expenses:

- ☐ How often do you or your staff catch taxis to meetings and what do these trips cost?

- ☐ How many phone calls do you and your staff make a day and how much do these cost?

- ☐ Are the lights left on in the office at the end of the day and how much does this cost?

- ☐ What are the miscellaneous items such as stationery, tea, coffee, milk, toilet paper and tissues costing your business each month? Are they being ordered in bulk, or purchased at the corner store? (You don't want to take them away — bah humbug! — just be aware of what's being spent.)

Getting the systems straight

Small business tends to be very entrepreneurial and fast moving, says Newstadt. And you don't want to burden your business with extra admin costs for the sake of tracking your costs. However, it's really hard to instil a cost-management culture if you can't keep an eye on the costs you're managing. 'You do need controls and proper processes in place to control expenditure', he adds. Set a limit on how much your employees can spend without getting you or a senior manager to sign off on it.

Of course, the amounts you decide on will depend on your business and the type of purchase you're talking about. 'Is it an ad hoc purchase such as a computer screen, or expenditure such as contract cleaning services?' asks Newstadt. 'You need to know if it is an asset that's being purchased or expenditure.' Sit down with your team and talk about the purchasing systems you currently have — what's working and what's not. By getting their input, you'll have more chance of a cost-management culture succeeding in your business. However, you then need to keep it going: making cost management the flavour of the month and then forgetting about it, Newstadt adds, will not do you, your staff or your business any favours.

On the subject of staff ...

Staff costs are fairly predictable. You know how many staff you have, what you pay them and when. You know they take holidays every year and how much this is going to cost your business (particularly if you need to replace them while they're away). What you don't have control over is someone leaving. Say a staffer resigns from your business tomorrow. Depending on how much notice this person has to give, you could have to pay out entitlements (of holidays and possibly time in lieu) in the next pay period, or the one after. Or maybe this person is retiring. Have you made cash provisions so that you can pay out accrued benefits? This, says Newstadt, is where problems often arise, especially for small business owners: 'You should always make sure you accrue these benefits, and be able to fund them, so you'll always be prepared'.

14 **Question:** *When is the best time to talk to the bank?*

Answer: *Keep your bank in the loop in the good times and the bad.*

Once upon a time, you knew more than your bank manager's name. You knew him personally, and thought nothing of inviting him out to lunch. Then banks started to centralise their business, and bank managers started to lose their cache. Loans were approved by head office. Problems were referred to telephone advisory centres. You still had a relationship with your bank, just not with the manager, who became more of an administrator than a relationship powerhouse. Times are now starting to change again, with some banks and non-bank lenders realising that their customers, including small businesses, want to feel more valued.

So now's a great time to make the most of your bank. First, look at it as a supplier. As with the other suppliers to your business, set up a good system of communication with your bank. This can begin before you've even started your business. Ask your local bank manager if he or she would have a look over your business plan. If the answer's no, get a business consultant or your accountant to go through it with you before you take it along to your bank. Even if the bank manager is unable to comment on it (for legal reasons) he or she will still like to see one. If your business has been up and running for a while, make an appointment and take in the facts of where you're at. Telling the manager about the highs and lows introduces your business well before you ever need to ask for anything.

Think like a bank

You might have to work at the communication, because the reality is that there's not a lot of return in dealing with small businesses for the banks. As Dr Graham Godbee of the Macquarie Graduate School of Management puts it in his book *Manage for All Seasons*: 'The old joke about banks is true: if you owe the bank $50 000 and cannot repay, you are in trouble; but if you owe the bank $500 million and cannot repay, then the bank is in trouble'.

The banking business is actually the risk management business. At the end of the day they're lending money to you based on a risk calculation:

→ Can you repay the loan?

→ Do you have the security if you can't repay the loan?

→ Where will the money be coming from on an ongoing basis?

Some of this information will come from your business plan. You might also have to supply them with a 12-month, 18-month or two-year projection of expected sales and expenditure. And don't forget your cash flow forecast: do you need to borrow $100 000 or $1 million?

Be proactive

How long have you been in business? What's the depth of management experience? Have your answers ready, advises Godbee, because your bank judges you as the owner on your knowledge of the business and any risks. This will all be punched into a computer, which then gives you a risk rating. However, don't wait until your business needs an injection of funds to start a discussion with your bank. Have your accounts and plans in good order. And then call some other banks, says Godbee. If your relationship with a bank is only worth a few hundreds of thousands of dollars in loans, he thinks you owe it to yourself to shop around (see breakout box below). 'Never just talk to one bank', he advises. 'Let them know you are looking around for the best deal.'

Action item: shopping around

Before you go talking to a few different banks, it helps to get your head around what you might need, and how they can help. There's a useful site that's been set up by the Australian Bankers' Association, called the Small Business Banking Portal <www.small businessbanking.com.au>. It offers free advice and information about banking solutions for the small business operator. It also lists an array of different banking products that are specifically aimed at small business in each state of Australia. You can shop around without even leaving your office.

Increase your value

To increase your value in the bank's eyes (so that if you do need them one day, they might listen), Godbee suggests bundling a whole range of your business's payment services, such as payroll, super, insurance and personal loans, through the one bank or lender. 'If you do this, make sure you also get quotes on what you'll pay for unbundling these services, in case you want to or have to in the future', he says. 'And get rid of any covenants: personal security and guarantees don't do your small business any favours.'

Be up with the Code

It's also worth being wised up on the Code of Banking Practice. The provisions of the Code were revised in 2004, and now include the bank–small business relationship (to read more, go to the Australian Bankers' Association's website <www.bankers.asn.au>, click on 'Industry Standards' and then 'ABA's Code of Banking Practice'). Basically, it talks about the banking sector's obligation to customers when it comes to standards of practice, disclosure and principles of conduct for their banking services.

However, Godbee says the best idea is to need less bank financing. Don't sit on too much stock; spend enough time chasing customers for payment. Even consider whether taking on an equity partner is an option. 'It's not something that a lot of small businesses ever consider', he adds. 'Most small businesses would prefer to have 100 per cent of $10 than 50 per cent of $1000.' Employee share ownership also could be a funding opportunity down the track, as opposed to the traditional bank route. The trick is to keep your mind open to options, have your accounts in good order and do your best to keep your bank in the loop.

Alternatives to banks

Don't just limit your investigations about finance to the major banks. There are other financial institutions that offer small businesses reliable financing. CPA Australia regularly updates a list of Australian financial institutions that offer lending products, including banks, building societies, credit unions and mortgage originators. You'll find the list as a PDF on the CPA website (go to <www.cpa australia.com.au>, click on 'Employment Sectors' then 'Small/Medium Businesses', then 'Managing Your Business' and 'Small business finance indicators'). Phone numbers and web addresses of all the lenders are in the PDF, so you can start finding out what they offer small businesses.

15

Question: *How much debt is it okay to have?*

Answer: *Financial leverage can be good for business, as long as you're aware of the risks you're taking on.*

If the most recent global financial meltdown has taught you anything, it's not to rely on your bank to set your level of small business debt. You need to be the master of your borrowings: know when to take on more debt, and when to reduce your risk. It's known as leverage (or gearing), and how much you do it in your business is a decision you shouldn't take lightly. Why? Because the more you borrow, the more highly geared your business will be. And this can have a significant impact on your level of success.

'Some leverage would help returns and may be still fairly safe, but too much leverage or gearing brings too much risk', says Dr Graham Godbee of the Macquarie Graduate School of

Management. All businesses go through their highs and lows; however, he says that highly geared companies have problems surviving the knocks. Even the major banks caution against highly leveraging a business. Yet the reality of growing your small business is that some debt *is* good.

The debt-versus-equity debate

Debt is an amount of money you borrow from a bank or lending institution. It's provided to you on specific terms and conditions, and you're expected to pay back the principal and the interest. Usually the lender will ask you to put up security in case you default on your payments. Equity, on the other hand, is the amount of value in your company — a share — that you give up to raise funds for your business. You might take on a partner, go into a joint venture or get a private investor involved.

The benefit of debt is that it can be easily accessed. All you have to do is support your application with facts about your business and a plan for how you'll pay back the money. Raising equity finance can be more involved because you have to find someone willing to invest in your business. Also, with debt finance you maintain ownership of your business. If there's any change in your business's fortunes, you still have to pay back the same amount of interest. When it comes to equity, you should also totally understand what you're giving up in return for an amount of money. And if you give up part of your equity now, what will this mean in a year or two?

The tax benefits

Another thing that gets thrown into this debate is the tax benefits of going into debt. When you borrow, the interest you pay is tax deductible under the Australian tax system. You can't claim the cost of equity as a deduction. This tax benefit, says Godbee, is known as the tax shield because it 'artificially gives a benefit to debt'. However, he cautions about getting too excited about the benefits of the tax shield because it's offset by the costs of bankruptcy. 'You do not need to go fully bankrupt to suffer the costs of bankruptcy', he says. 'Once the company is in trouble, the banks start to raise interest rates, put in more restrictive loan covenants, the company loses the ability to pick up good opportunities, the banks may even insist on asset disposals, unfavourable equity issues and so on.'

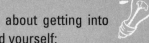

Action item: question time

Before talking to your bank about getting into debt, make sure you've asked yourself:

- How much money will the business need?

- How will this money be used?

- How will this finance help the business meet a market demand?

- How will the loan be repaid?

- What will the business look like in the future as a result of this finance?

Source: ANZ Bank small business portal <www.anz.com/small-business/>.

Mind your risk

There are two types of business risk: operational and financial. According to Godbee, most people see operational risk as the things that can go wrong in your business, including competitor activity, equipment breakdown and default by a major customer. However, he thinks a better way to think of operational risk is to consider how volatile your cash flows are. On the flipside is financial risk. This includes commitments such as debt, long-term leases, insurance cover and the hedging you do on things such as exchange rates. All these are a burden when sales, profits and cash flow drop, adds Godbee. To manage the burden, he suggests you look at your risk mix.

Little or no debt

You can operate your business with no debt and no risk: everything's insured and hedged, and you use your own capital reserves instead of debt to pay for any growth. However, Godbee points out that it's probably too conservative because you won't have the leverage to grow, and you won't get the tax shield because you don't have debt. Instead, he advises going for a mix of low operations risk (using stable and predictable cash flows) to service a higher finance risk (higher levels of debt), while also possibly utilising less insurance and hedging. 'The better returns may justify the increase in risk', he says.

Lots of debt

This can be your no-sleep-at-night kind of strategy, and one that Godbee doesn't think makes any sense for small business owners. You combine high operations risk with high finance risk. 'You may get away with it for some years while the operating cash flows are above the financial commitments', he says. 'You and others may then think you are a brilliant manager or investor. But it is only a matter of time before reality hits, tough times return and operating cash flows fall below the financial commitments.' Even the banks get worried when you start contemplating this sort of high–high risk strategy.

Some debt

Combing a higher operations risk (where you allow your cash flow to be more volatile) with a low finance risk makes the most sense, according to Godbee. 'While management will still do what it can to reduce operational risk, it cannot remove all the risks (such as competitor activity and equipment breakdown) in a viable manner. So a conservative financial policy reduces the fixed commitments to service debt, while insurance and hedging are used extensively to further offset the operations risk', he says. 'Earnings will be reduced because of the extra costs associated with the conservative financial policy but this is done to improve the chances for long-term survival.'

Back to basics

The best way to think about debt is as a service to your business, not the be-all of your whole business. The real value of a business, according to Godbee, is in the earning capacity of your assets and your ability as the boss to achieve the earnings. If you're wondering how much debt is right for your business, first work out your expected future cash flow (see more on this in question 10). Take the time to look closely at the stability or volatility of these figures. And keep going back to them, revising them if you have to from year to year. Don't go into debt just to pay for shortfalls in your cash flow. If the numbers don't add up, it's probably because they really don't add up. Accept the sign and take the softly, softly approach.

16 Question: *What about overdrafts and loans?*

Answer: *Choose your short–term finance wisely.*

We all know money makes money. And some debt can be good. When you're in small business, there also are times when all you need is a financial leg-up to help you over that cash-flow hurdle or to purchase equipment that will launch you into the next stage of success. Banks are in the business of supplying you with lots of different products that aim to help. They make money out of them. But they are also in the business of managing their own risk. And they can turn the cash taps down, or even switch them off, when money is tight (and small business owners are often the first to suffer).

That's why you should go into any lending relationship with your eyes wide open. Know your options. Never be desperate. Every bank and non-bank business lender does want to loan you money within reason. As long as you can show them you know what you're doing, and that you're not going to be too big a risk for their business, you're in with a chance. Know your financing options and why you want a particular one. You'll be in a better position to make sensible decisions on the sort of lending products you do and don't need.

Overdrafts

Overdrafts are a short-term finance facility that can prop up your business when your seasonal cash flow is low (for example, for two or three months of the year), or so you can buy that piece of equipment that will help you generate more money for your business. Security is usually required (although you can get unsecured overdrafts, which are charged at higher rates of interest), and the bank will put your business through a credit assessment. Every overdraft has a limit, and if you go over this limit you'll be penalised default interest (which could be up to 6 per cent of the overdraft). Always go into an overdraft knowing exactly how much you want and why you want it.

'If an overdraft is a true overdraft and it's being used in the correct way in your business, it should reach zero, or be close to it, at some point through the year', says Dr Graham Godbee of the Macquarie Graduate School of Management. 'You will pay a line fee on the amount of the overdraft limit even though you may not borrow to the limit.' So don't go into an overdraft with just a rough guess of how much money you're going to need. And never overestimate the amount: it's a line of credit, and you should use it wisely like any other form of credit. Also remember that the overdraft can be called in by the bank at any time (in dire circumstances this could be with just 24 hours' notice, although most banks would prefer to reduce your overdraft if they needed the money rather than take it all away). 'Unfortunately, banks tend to call in the overdraft when businesses are most vulnerable: when the bank has detected a weakness in the business or during a credit squeeze', says Godbee.

Once you have an overdraft, how you use it is a smoke signal of how you run your business. 'If your overdraft is at or close to its limit most of the time, bankers have a term for it: hardcore overdraft', he cautions. 'It is a warning that the business is stretching its finances and requires better financial management.' If this is you, or you can see that you would probably work at or near your overdraft limit, you'd be better off considering another type of funding for your business.

Loans

When the money you need in your business is for longer term needs, you can shop around for finance, whether it's a term loan, line of credit (also known as an equity loan) or fully drawn advance. These products give you access to funds, although lenders usually like to earmark them for capital investment in your business. A line of credit is secured against a registered mortgage on a property, and fully drawn advances are secured against residential or commercial property. Because both these finance options are backed by property that you or your business owns, the interest charged is less than for an overdraft. What you should find out, however, is the fees you'll be charged if you don't use the line of credit facility. And if you were to default on the payments (for the principal and/or interest of the loan amount), could you lose your house, office or factory?

Action item: business loan finder

The Australian Government's business portal <www.business.gov.au> offers a free business loan calculator (click on 'How-to-guides', then

Action item *(cont'd)*: business loan finder

'Starting a business', then 'How can I find a business loan'. Just type in how much money you need, whether you need it at call or upfront (and how long you'll need to pay it back), if you're looking at fixed or variable interest and what type of security you're willing to put up. The calculator will actually find you different bank and non-bank lenders with products to suit your business finance enquiry.

Know what you want and why

Doing your research is the key. Always understand the fees and charges on every loan you're contemplating. Is the interest fixed or variable? What are the penalties if you don't make a payment on time? Have a firm idea of how much money you want, and why (don't over- or underestimate this amount). What security are you putting up? And how does your cash flow and business plan support your loan application? Remember, a bank or non-bank lender will usually only reject your application if they don't have confidence in your ability to repay the loan, if your cash flow is way out of whack or if you haven't given them enough information to prove your operation is worth the lending risk. So before you sign on the dotted line, have a clear plan for the money. It's also worth passing your loan application by your accountant to check.

Cashing in on credit cards

A credit card can be a useful finance tool for small business, depending on what sort of business you're in and the set-up of your operation, says Dr Graham Godbee. Like overdrafts, they offer your business a short-term cash solution. Unlike overdrafts or formal loans they can be approved quickly, without having to provide 12-month business forecasts, and they have a lower fee structure, or no fees. You can utilise the interest-free period on your card, and get the benefit of bonus points if the card is tied to a loyalty or frequent flyer program. Just keep an eye on the interest you're paying if you don't pay the balance off in full within the interest-free period. Godbee advises you to always pay off the credit card in full each month: 'Don't have them maxed out because it's the most expensive form of interest'.

17 **Question:** *My family has put cash in to my business. How much should I tell them about the day-to-day business stuff?*

Answer: *It's all about managing expectations, as you would with any investor.*

Families can be wonderful things. They believe in you no matter what, and come to your rescue throughout life. Now that you've set up your business, they've even offered to help you out financially so that you can get over an upcoming hurdle, or to boost your business into its growth phase. The crunch can come, however, when they also want to know the ins and outs of your operation, or to have more of a say in how you run things.

What you have to decide, as the business owner, is how happy you are to have others in your business bed with you. Look at your family as you would any outside investor. They've put cash in, so they have every right to want to know what's going on in your business. The difference between a great owner–investor relationship and one that leaves a bad taste in everyone's mouth, however, comes down to expectations.

Family first

An offer of financial help from your family mostly comes from the heart. They care about you, and they want your business to be successful. However, it pays to have some pretty thorough business discussions with your family *before* you take their money. How do they see it working? How much do they want to be involved? How much do they expect in return for their investment? Will you be happy with all this? Setting out everyone's expectations from the start, and writing it all down, can help if things get more complicated down the track. Or if your business grows even more and there's a bigger pie to share.

An important part of your discussion with your family should be about everyone's get-out clause. If your family members suddenly need their money, how will you give it to them? How much return will you give them on their initial investment? What if things don't work out? Think about it all from a rational business perspective, not an emotional one. Your future Merry Christmases are counting on it.

Get some good advice

Getting your solicitor to draw up the legal structure of the business will help clarify what everyone wants out of the deal. This usually comes in the form of a Shareholders' Agreement. It could include how the financials are going to be managed. Or you could ask your accountant to handle the financials separately. The best thing about using these professionals is that they don't have the emotional attachment to your family or your business that you do, and they often can see things that you won't. (If you don't have a good accountant or a solicitor, go to question 7 for tips on finding one.)

Action item: online exercise

Canberra BusinessPoint <www.canberrabus inesspoint.com.au> is an online advisory initiative from the ACT Government and supported by Deloitte. The site offers a comprehensive, and free, e-learning module that anyone in a family business, or with family investors, should take the time to do. There's even a section on the 'Separation of Business and Personal Wealth'. Simply register online and then go to 'E-learning Programs', then 'Business Basics 2', then 'The Family Owned Business'. Do the quiz at the end of the module and see how well you've planned your family in to your business.

Know your goals

If you're accepting any type of investment in your business, you need to have a good long look at why you want the money in the first place. Which of your business goals will it help bring alive? Dr Graham Godbee writes in *Manage for All Seasons* that these goals are wide-ranging and can include 'performance, robustness (being able to withstand the bad times), opportunism, flexibility, independence and importance, and time—not so much free time but more control over time'. Once you've identified your business goals and written them down, you'll have a better idea of how you'll use an investor's money to achieve one or more of them. Investors are entitled to know your plans, too. Whether a formal investor or your family, you should be able to demonstrate how well you operate things and your vision for the future. Be ready with your written list.

The investment motivators

When it comes to family investment, it's often a desire to help that drives the actions of your nearest and dearest. Other types of investors, such as venture capitalists and shareholders, aren't so interested in the warm and fuzzies of your business. They just demand information on how their investment is performing: what sort of returns are they getting, and should they stick with bankrolling your business?

Then there are investors known as business angels: private backers who are matched with small businesses and then provide them with funds and expertise for a financial return. According to Christine Kaine, founder of the company Business Angels Pty Ltd <www.businessangels.com.au>, business angels are a bit different from normal investors because they're motivated to give something back to the community. Unlike investment from family members, the business angel contributes expertise and skills to a business. 'Many investors say that businesses are not clear about the way ahead and think that money is the answer to their problems', says Kaine. 'Think about things from the investor's point of view, not just your business point of view.'

Managing expectations

This is probably where a lot of investment relationships, whether it's with your family, a friend or a total stranger, come unstuck. Everyone has their expectations in their head. But people aren't mind readers: poor communication can sink your potential for success. Christine Kaine recommends that you ask your accountant or solicitor to put together watertight partnership agreements for every investment deal. Not only will it lay down each partner's expectations in black and white, it will give you a clear 'mechanism for dispute resolution and a schedule for continual business plan review'. Call it your insurance policy.

18 **Question:** *Are government grants just an urban myth?*

Answer: *They really do exist; you just have to know where to look for them.*

It's sort of like winning the lottery. Or being given a bonus by the tooth fairy. Only better, because landing a government grant is all about your business, and the fact that someone else believes in its future. However, businesses that do win a government grant seem to be a bit of an urban myth. You've heard about them, but you've never met the lucky souls who've scored. That's possibly because they're so exhausted from trawling through government websites and filling out grant applications that they can't speak, let alone broadcast to the world that they've snared money from the government's treasure-trove.

Every year the federal and state governments give out billions of dollars in grants and subsidies. Small business owners are often eligible to capture some of this money; however, the whole process of finding and applying for a government grant is often plonked in your too-hard basket. Knowing where to look in the first place is the key. Then your success can rely on how you put your application together and prove that you meet the funding criteria. There are industry-specific websites you can visit for information on the types of grants that are available in your sector. As well, each state and territory government has a department of economic or business development that has reams of information about the state-centric grants that are available each year.

For export grants, you also can head to the Austrade site <www.austrade.gov.au> for information on assistance if you're looking to take your product or service overseas (for more details on harnessing export opportunities, see question 45). And then there are the many different federal government grants on offer every year (the main information sites for these national programs are listed on pp. 79–80).

Why you get grants

Money isn't usually given out for working capital or to start a business. However, one-off capital projects, business expansion, training, research and development, export assistance and innovation all rate highly in the grants grab. What you have to remember, as the potential recipient of a grant, is that governments don't just give their money out to anyone. You have to be seen as being worthy of the financial boost. The committees selecting grant recipients want proof.

What you need

Make sure you have a comprehensive business plan and sound financial records to demonstrate the viability of your business. You might need to explain your vision for your business and why this grant will help you get there. While the sorts of grants your business is eligible for will depend on what you do, and how you do it, it's often the standard of your application that will get you noticed. So spend the time checking out the following sites, and get your supporting information in order. After all, you've got to be in it to win it!

Action item: how to apply

Grant applications are all different; however, there are certain things to know before you go filling in the forms.

◻ Research the selection criteria, and how your business is eligible.

- ▫ Tick off the grant requirements and get together all supporting material to back up your application.

- ▫ Make sure your finances are correct, and your rationale for receiving the stash of money is sound.

- ▫ Demonstrate how your business is 'ready to go': that you have what it takes to implement the actions once you receive the grant.

- ▫ Be patient, as once you submit your grant application it might take weeks to hear if you're in with a chance.

<www.business.gov.au>

This site is probably the largest guide to the huge number of government grants on offer in Australia. It also contains information on and links to state and territory government grant authorities. There are agricultural and business development grants, business grants for women, drought assistance grants, employment and environmental grants and indigenous and start-up grants listed on the Grant Finder part of the site (click on 'Grants & assistance' in the 'Business topics' box on the home page). Narrowing down your search on this site will certainly save you a heap of time.

<www.innovation.gov.au>

The Australian Government's Department of Innovation, Industry, Science and Research has put this site together. While it has a definite slant towards innovation, research and development, under the 'Programs & Services' section of the site you'll find a brief summary on a large selection of government programs and schemes. Many of them are designed to assist small business. Click on the link for each specific grant in the list and you'll be forwarded to another part of the site, or an external site, for more information.

<www.ausindustry.gov.au>

AusIndustry is another arm of the Department of Innovation, Industry, Science and Research. On its website at the time of writing, 43 government programs, including a few grants programs for small business, were listed (click on 'Small Business' under 'AusIndustry Programs' on the home page). Some are merit-based, some are specifically for capital projects and some highlight the concessions your business can get when it comes to different duties and taxes. To find out more, you're advised to contact AusIndustry directly on 13 28 46 or email <hotline@ausindustry.gov.au>.

<www.grantslink.gov.au>

Created by the Australian Government's Department of Infrastructure, Transport, Regional Development and Local Government, GrantsLINK is worth checking out because there are over 250 government grants and funding programs linked to the Find A Grant section of the site. All of the grants are federal, state or local government sponsored (they have to have a .gov.au domain to be on the site). It's a bit of a one-stop shop for grant seekers. Depending on your industry or business sector, and the sort of grant you're looking for, you simply enter particular keywords into the site search and the results are found for you.

Part III

Managing your people power

This section encompasses the ins and outs of people management. Whether you want to hire, fire or get the most out of your existing talent, it offers proven strategies to make your people management life easier.

A vibrant small business often comes down to those who work in it. Knowing how to hire great people is a start. Being able to effectively manage them will create a dynamic workplace culture, regardless of whether your business employs one or 20 people. Get the people side of things right and your business will thrive, even if you're not there!

19

Question: *Are there any tricks to hiring great people?*

Answer: *Focus on the type of person who will fit with your business culture.*

What makes a great employee? Obviously, it depends on your business and what you need them to do. If you need a widget maker, they have to know widgets. A manager has to be able to get along with people. However, what you want to find is someone who wants to work in small business; someone who wants to work in *your* small business.

People have a strong preference on the size of firms they want to work for, according to Professor Ian Williamson, professor of management at Melbourne Business School. Some people enjoy the fact that they can get exposure to a wide variety of jobs. 'They can have an impact on the business. Small business should highlight this when they are recruiting', he says. Focus on the basic competencies you want from someone in your business. Williamson suggests asking: is the person conscientious and do they have the intelligence to learn and adapt?

Where to start

Before you even write a job ad, it's a good idea to take a step back and look at what you want a new person to do. Write down a job description. The Australian Government site <www.business.gov.au> states that by defining the responsibilities and functions of a job, you can more easily pinpoint the knowledge, experience and skills that you need. If you're stuck on what to write, have a look at the weekend newspaper and see what other businesses are writing in the employment classifieds: how do they describe a similar sort of job? You can then use the job description document as the basis of appraisals when they start with you (see more on this in question 21). If you don't have something written down and set aside a time once a year to go through it, how are you going to know if someone has done a good job for you or not?

Quick tips

If you're in the recruiting wilderness, Business Victoria <www.business.vic.gov.au> has some good recruiting tips on its website (click on 'Starting & Managing a Business', followed by 'Employing & Managing Staff' then 'Recruiting Staff'). If you're looking for ways to write a job ad, the University of Technology Sydney's HR department gives you a snapshot of the essential ingredients on its website (<www.hru.uts.edu.au/recruitment>; click on 'Recruiting staff', then 'Attracting candidates' then 'Writing good adverts').

Finding good people

The thought of going through the whole hiring process can be daunting, particularly if you've never done it before. Just remember that your business will only be as good as the people you employ. So take the time to find people with the right fit.

Here are a few ways you can find them:

→ *People you know.* A lot of small business's vacancies are filled because you know someone who'd be right for the job. It could be a friend, family member or sporting buddy. Your network can be a handy way to build your team: like-minded people do have a good dynamic. Just remember that you're not always going to know someone who's right for one of your jobs. So set up the interview and hiring processes now so you can benefit when your business gets bigger.

→ *Poaching people.* This is when you target other businesses in your industry sector and contact their good staff to see if they're interested in a change. The plus is that you get trained talent who know your type of business. The minus happens if the person is still loyal to his or her old job, or your customers still associate them with their former employer. Make sure you're ready for the fallout before you attempt to poach staff.

→ *Unsolicited CVs*. There are times when you might get a CV sent to you from someone you don't know. It's always worth having a look at them and filing the interesting ones away for the future. When you're ready to hire, get the CVs out and contact anyone you think is worth interviewing. At least you know they've been proactive in their job hunting.

→ *Placing an ad*. A job ad, either in a local or capital city newspaper, or trade journal, states what the job is and who should apply. Be careful with the wording: the Australian Government's website <www.business.gov.au> says that, by law, you can't use 'discriminatory language that may exclude potential employees on the basis of race, age, sex, marital status, family status or responsibility, pregnancy, religious and political beliefs, disability, gender history or sexual orientation'. Use bullet points in the ad and include your contact details and a cut-off date for applications. Don't accept any applications after this date (what would they be like at work if they can't get a CV in on time?).

→ *Going online*. You can find great staff by posting an ad on the internet. The trick is to know the most effective place to put it. Start at the Australian Government's JobSearch initiative website <www.jobsearch.gov.au/employerinfo/>. It offers small businesses free job advertising with a high online search ranking (it usually lists on the first page of Google job searches) plus it has a heap of workforce and recruitment information.

→ *Professional recruiters.* To help you cast the biggest net you can, particularly if you've exhausted all your networks, you could enlist the services of a third-party recruiter. 'Small businesses lack a reputation in a broader community of potential talent, so hiring from formal channels can be beneficial', says Williamson. Recruitment companies also have formal procedures that you'll be able to tap into during your search for the perfect candidate. Just make sure you choose one that understands your business.

What to look for in a CV

It takes recruiters no more than a minute to work out whether a curriculum vitae or résumé will go on the interview pile or not. What do they look for?

▫ *A CV that sells the applicant's skills.* It shouldn't just be a rundown of the applicant's life experience, but more of a marketing document that tells you instantly why you need this person. Has he or she put the most relevant skills for the job up high? Does the CV layout look professional? If it's handwritten and the job ad stated typing skills were needed, it's a quick way to rule this person out.

▫ *A CV that tells you something about his or her personality.* Is it accurate (with no spelling mistakes), clear (bullet points) and dynamic with the latest buzz words and industry jargon? Do you want this sort of person in your organisation?

▫ *A CV that says why he or she wants to work for you.* Has this person even bothered to look at your website or drive past your business to see what you're like? If the applicant has shown that he or she has done some research on you and your competitors, this person probably really does want to work for you.

The interview

Small businesses often run fairly informal interviews, but that doesn't mean they should be sloppy. List all your questions, and ask everyone you interview the same things. Identify the tasks the person will need to do, and work out a way to get applicants to demonstrate their ability during the interview. For example, if they need computer competencies, have a computer set up so they can show you their skills. 'What you should be doing is using other tests besides interviews; for example, personality tests and work samples', says Williamson. 'They may make the interview process a little longer, but a bad hiring decision is a death knell for small business.'

Phone a friend

Having someone you trust sit in on the interview can provide you with an additional perspective: an impartial set of eyes and ears. He or she might pick up on different things, and will be a great sounding board for you when you're trying to decide which candidate would be best for your organisation. 'You should go into the process with some level of sophistication, as in the other domains of your business. Your level of attention with this is your indicator of success', adds Williamson.

20 **Question:** *Why is firing someone such a drama?*

Answer: *Emotion often gets in the way of fair play when things don't work out with staff.*

Having to fire a staff member rates right up there as one of the most stressful experiences any business owner has to go through. You run through, over and over again, how you're going to approach it. This person hasn't been performing and you know he or she is not right for your business. This person needs to go. But you don't have a human resources department to deal with disgruntled employees. You're it.

There's a multitude of ways to handle it. The best one: concentrate on being fair. You'll significantly reduce the stress of showing a staffer the door by thinking about fair play through the whole process. 'How you handle things in a small business is more important for the people staying than for the one going', says Professor Ian Williamson, professor of management at Melbourne Business School. 'That's where the (small business) qualities of transparency, clarity and fairness come into their own.'

Write it down

Keeping records from the moment you start hiring staff is essential if you want to protect yourself from legal flair-ups in the future (see more on this following). Don't think that just because you get along well with your team when you hire them that it will always be this way. Keep records on their performance, as well as your expectations. It doesn't have to be hugely formal, but the documentation does have to be there. Give your staff annual performance appraisals and give them a copy so that you both know how they're tracking. 'Write down specific goals, targets and what they've done well', says Williamson. 'Having documentation associated with these things takes the emotion out and gives you grounds on which to stipulate fair warnings. There's a perceived fairness and it makes managing staff easier.'

Know the law

New fair dismissal laws took effect in Australia on 1 July 2009. They are of particular relevance to small businesses with fewer than 15 full-time equivalent employees, according to the Australian Government's Department of Education, Employ-ment and Workplace Relations <www.deewr.gov.au>.

(From 1 January 2011 the new laws will apply to small businesses with fewer than 15 employees based on actual headcount rather than the equivalent of full-time employee hours.) Under these laws, employees can't make a claim of unfair dismissal until they have been with you for a year (up from six months under the old laws), and a Fair Dismissal Code has been put in place for employers to refer to in any dispute. The Fair Dismissal Code is all about providing employers and employees with a fair and reasonable process for sorting out any workplace issue that might end in dismissal (for a rundown of how to access the Code, see the breakout box below).

As an employer, you no longer have to give an employee multiple warnings or put a warning in writing (although it's recommended that you do in case you need to refer to a particular conversation in the future). You'll be operating within the law as long as you give a valid reason for the potential dismissal (based on his or her conduct or ability to do the work), and offer a reasonable chance to improve performance. You need to act fairly and reasonably in these reviews.

Action item: fair dismissal checklist

The Department of Education, Employment and Workplace Relations <www.deewr.gov.au> has a Small Business Fair Dismissal Code Checklist (click on 'Workplace Relations' followed by 'Australia's New Workplace Relations System', then 'Resources' and 'Program Fact Sheets'). Go to the site and print it out. Then if you ever have a potential dismissal issue, you can fill it out at the same time you're discussing things with your employee. It pays to file any paperwork like this in one spot just in case you ever need to refer to it in the future.

Being fair and reasonable

This often comes down to communication. Not just when there's conflict, but all the time. If you have an open system of communication with your team, there are no surprises. Make the time to sit down with each of your employees for an hour at some point in the year and discuss how they're going. If you're not happy, let them know in a constructive way: stick to the facts and keep the emotion out of it.

'It's easy to skip this in a small business because you can see them every day', says Williamson. 'As you grow it becomes more critical because you may not see them all every day, but you want them performing for you. So set the expectations from the start.' Make the communication direct and professional. And know the difference between interpersonal conflict and job performance or work-related conflict. 'If people act in a disruptive manner there has to be reprimand in that', adds Williamson. 'But it's up to you to have set the guidelines down for the culture of your business.'

Managing conflict

You don't have to love everyone you employ. But you have to respect them, and they have to respect you. Treat employees fairly and word will get out that your business is a good place to work. And you'll probably have less conflict than other businesses around you. If you do have conflict with an employee, keep your cool. Be direct. Let the employee know he or she has stepped over the line. Ask how the situation could be changed. Are you happy with this person's ideas? Respond, and give the improvement process a time frame. Then review it together. Things don't always work out with employees, but it's important you let the employee maintain dignity through the whole process. Manage it calmly and efficiently, and have the documentation as a backup. Then, if there is ill will when you let this person go, at least you know you've done the best you can for you, this person and your business.

If things flair up

Sometimes an employee won't be happy with being fired, no matter how reasonable you think you've been. That's why the Australian Government has set up a mediation office called Fair Work Australia. According to the Department of Education, Employment and Workplace Relations, an unfair dismissal claim should be lodged within 14 days with Fair Work Australia, which acts as the 'independent umpire' to help sort things out in workplaces around the country.

Fair Work Australia officers will investigate the facts of a dispute. That's why it's great for you to have written everything down. The Fair Work officer will hold informal talks with you and your former employee. The idea is to mediate an out-of-court solution that's in the best interests of everyone involved. For more information go to <www.fairwork.gov.au> or call 13 13 94. Ask one of the Fair Work advisers what they think. It's in the interests of your employees who are left behind that you get it right.

21 **Question:** *How can I make my staff feel valuable, without paying them more?*

Answer: *Look at the way you motivate your team.*

When was the last time you went out of your way to make someone in your team feel good about working for you? If your answer is 'last week', you're obviously into motivation, but there might be more you could do. If your answer is 'can't remember', and your team building is ad hoc at best, there are definite things you can do to make your workplace somewhere that people want to be. If your team building is akin to the pharaoh syndrome ('my staff should be thankful they have a job'), then now's the time to lift your game before your pyramid comes tumbling down.

'The research on this is clear', says Professor Ian Williamson of Melbourne Business School. 'Positive social interaction is core to peoples' work value and identity.' This happens at a really basic level, and people vary on the importance they place on it. 'Essentially they have to appreciate the benefits they get out of your business or they will leave', he adds.

Team dynamics

While you probably can't pay your employees the same sort of money they could get in larger organisations, you have the power to create a great team. Williamson calls this the social environment of a small business. You *can* share your goals for the business with your staff. You *can* get them on board your unique business proposition. 'The onus is on you to get the input from your team, and respond to it', says Williamson.

Your team is the arms and legs, heart and soul of your business. Often they're on your frontline with customers and clients. Even if they're not, they still perform some sort of task you need in your product or service delivery. A drop in morale can impact on your bottom line because people who feel unappreciated don't work so well. They start to think that if the boss doesn't care about them, why should they care about the boss and the business? So get in first and open up the communication channels with your staff. Make time for more formal monthly team chats. Sit down with each staffer and write out their job descriptions, and praise them on the things they do well. If the communication lines are always open, your employees will feel appreciated and respected.

Flexible success

As the boss, it's important that you always keep in mind why you set up your business in the first place. Then bring this vision into your management of your team. 'Call it the rules of engagement', says Williamson. 'Small firms benefit from the fact that they are often set up with the aim of providing flexibility and they also have the ability to adapt better than large organisations. They should use this advantage in every aspect of the business.'

Doing this comes down to your ability to motivate your team. Here are some tips:

→ Think about rotating roles within the team. It gives everyone a fresh sense of how they fit into your big picture, and helps them appreciate what everyone else does.

→ Every month, ask your team for their suggestions on how you can do things better. You might be surprised by what comes out of a positive brainstorming session.

→ Let everyone know that you've created an adaptable and flexible workplace. For example, what sort of flexibility would they like instead of a $5000 pay rise?

→ Lead by example: go home early some days, and try to always be available to go along to your child's award presentation. Allow your team to do the same. Creating an environment that doesn't just pay lip-service to the notion of work–life balance is a great motivator for staff.

→ Think outside the square of how you can motivate others. To get you started, check out the free *Ways to Motivate* template provided by the Tasmanian Government's Department of Economic Development and Tourism (go to <www.development.tas.gov.au/betterworkplaces> and click on 'Motivate, Manage & Reward Performance').

The benefits to your bottom line

Staff training is something a lot of small businesses don't do, often because of a lack of either finance or time. But if your business doesn't invest in its people, they will leave. Training doesn't have to cost a lot, and the payback you'll get will be multiplied. According to research quoted on the Australian

Government web portal <www.training.com.au>, staff who receive formal training can be 230 per cent more productive than untrained colleagues who are working in the same role. And a business that invests in targeted training can have an increase in labour productivity by as much as a 30 per cent return on their investment. If you don't believe it, you can actually measure this multiplication with the site's Return on Investment Calculator (check it out in the breakout box below).

Of course, the type of training you opt for will depend on what your business and staff need. Which extra skills would course X give your team? How will this impact your bottom line? Professor Ian Williamson says that everything you do, including training your staff, should go back to the tangible benefits to your business. So spend the money wisely. Think about the advantages for your business if your staff learn new technology, or get up-to-date industry information in specific areas of their jobs. 'Don't make training an entitlement, it's an investment', he says. 'Plan how you're going to evaluate the benefits to your business-related outcomes: is it on your customers, your production or your processes?'

Action item: Return on Investment Calculator

If you're going to spend money on training, make sure you measure its success in terms of what it does for your business's bottom line. The Australian Government's web portal <www.training.com.au> offers a free Return on Investment Calculator (you'll find the ROI Calculator in the 'Business and Employers' section of the site). It will actually calculate your costs of training versus the perceived benefits to your business. Check it out before you spend a cent on any type of training.

Training options

Once you decide what you need, there are many training options, such as vocational education courses (certificates or diplomas), free workshops and seminars. As a start, have a look at the list of upcoming free seminars sponsored by the federal government at <www.business.gov.au/events>. You also should check out the list of licensed training providers at the National Training Information Service's website <www.ntis.gov.au>. Other courses can be accessed through your local TAFE college or private training organisations. And your nearest Business Enterprise Centre (go to <www.beca.org.au>) often hosts business training and workshops.

Take a moment to think about the opportunity cost of not spending some money on training your staff: if they leave you'll lose vital skills and knowledge, and it'll take time and money to recruit someone new. On the other hand, if you spend money on training and education, your employees will feel good about themselves and about your company, and this will have a positive impact on the way they work and communicate to customers. A definite win–win.

22 **Question:** *Is there any real benefit to mentoring?*

Answer: *It can give you real, measurable business benefits.*

Are leaders born or bred? Anyone who's ever worked with a business visionary knows that some people have the L-factor (leadership factor) when it comes to rallying their troops. Others have to work at it. Regardless of where you fall on the management spectrum, you can still create something great by making the concept of leadership an essential element of your small business offering from day one. Imparting your vision to the people around you will help you all strive for the same goals. Your staff will believe in you, and so will your clients.

But what if you then take yourself out of the equation? Would the inspiring vibe you've created fall apart? Have you ever thought of supporting others in your business to step up and take the lead? By introducing the concept of mentoring into your workplace, you'll be inspiring staff to inspire each other. When you're not there, your business continues to thrive because everyone wants it to.

What is mentoring?

Mentoring is different from coaching. A mentor is someone who guides you through your professional growth. A coach is someone who assists you in a specific task or skill and follows up to make sure it's happened. The difference is that a coach knows where you should be on the playing field, and works with you to get you to that spot, while a mentor lets you set the direction and make the decisions, supporting you the whole way. A mentor is someone you trust and who can give you advice, or just be your sounding board.

A mentor for you as the boss could be someone with more business experience who's prepared to guide you through your entrepreneurial adventure. This person will share their ups and downs with you, and give you tips when you need them. Sometimes it will be someone you meet along your business journey. You realise instantly that you trust his or her judgement and can learn from his or her experience. Your mentor will usually offer this knowledge for free, getting a kick out of seeing you succeed.

If you've never found anyone you think would make a good mentor to you, there are formal mentoring programs around Australia. Usually the programs offer the services of retired businesspeople who have a wealth of experience. Often they're volunteers and it's the service that charges you a fee to bring you together (for example, there's one in Victoria called the Small Business Mentoring Service, which charges $75 to $100 per mentoring session — for details go to <www.sbms.org.au>).

However, it doesn't just have to be you, the boss, being mentored. Vibrant small businesses look to mentoring for their team as an important part of their strategic plan. 'Small businesses have an advantage in that the intimacy of their interaction facilitates mentoring', says Professor Ian Williamson, professor of management at Melbourne Business School. He believes it's beneficial because 'it leverages the intrinsic and emotional qualities fostered in small business'. It can happen informally or as a structured program (see breakout box below). The benefit of having some sort of structure is that you can then measure how it's going. 'Have the formally articulated conversation and then let the experience of mentoring create something great', suggests Williamson. To find out how great, it's a good idea to review your mentoring every year. Over the page are just a few of the positives you can expect to get out of mentoring.

Action item: mentoring program 101

Setting up a structured mentoring program doesn't have to be difficult. Look at it as an investment in your biggest resource: your people.

❑ *What's in it?* Set the purpose of the mentoring (why you're doing it). This might include providing a sounding board through the use of someone who's been there before. Let your team help create the goals of the program so that they buy in to it. Work out if you'll need any extra resources (external volunteers perhaps?). Stipulate that it's a confidential process and give staff a 'get out' clause if it's not working. Cover your legal responsibilities to OH&S and ethical issues by going through the dos and don'ts of the mentoring relationship.

Action item *(cont'd)*: mentoring program 101

▫ *How often should you do it?* Organise a regular time once a week initially and then as required (but at least once a month) for the mentor and mentee to get together. Give the program three months to run and then review how it's going and whether the benefits are being realised.

▫ *How do you measure it?* Get feedback from the mentor and mentee on how successful they think the program has been. Constantly review the objective of why you're meeting and if the meetings are achieving what everyone wants them to.

▫ *Where to get information?* Mentoring Australia, the national association of mentors, has a checklist you can utilise (while it's aimed more at corporates, it will give you a good overview of the process). Go to the link at <www.dsf.org.au/resources/detail/?id=22>.

Mentoring develops team spirit

If your team is working well together, your business will hum. However, often team spirit doesn't just happen. You have to work at it. Mentoring is one way to help it along. 'Because you're engaging people at an individual level, there is staff satisfaction, improvements in client relationships and there are decreases in productivity issues and issues surrounding staff', says Williamson. A basic human quality is to want to feel like you're part of something bigger than yourself. So why not create this kind of culture in your business? Sit down with your team and together set yourselves some objectives for a mentoring program. What can you mentor them in? How can they guide you? Can your team mentor each other? Work out a way to make team spirit happen: you're all on the bus together, so you may as well enjoy the trip.

Mentoring boosts your business IP

Your business is only as good as the people in it. Often when employees leave a small business, particularly if they've been working for you for a while, they take a lot of intellectual property (IP) with them. A mentoring program can help make sure you're not left high and dry, and to guarantee that your IP isn't tied to an individual. 'It allows for the cross-fertilisation of ideas', says Williamson. As the mentor, you can provide the expertise that helps all staff develop their confidence and achieve some positive outcomes for your business. 'The cost can be minimal as a way to enhance staff qualifications', he adds. To make it as cost effective as you can, be a bit creative about the type of mentoring you engage in: you can even think about utilising professional associations as sources of external mentors for your team. All this will further enhance the intellectual property in your business.

Mentoring motivates staff

Mentoring is all about creating an atmosphere of advice and support in your business. Once your staff know this, they'll be even bigger fans. 'It enhances the professional standing of employees and probably enhances your reputation by the way it's perceived', says Williamson. Your employees notice that you're doing them a favour and they respond in a supportive way. They'll be motivated to stay working for you because you believe in the importance of developing them to their potential. You're also empowering them to make informed decisions to grow your business.

Mentoring opens up communication

What do your people want to get out of working for you? What do you expect in return? The establishment of some sort of formal mentoring can help you start these conversations. Suddenly, you open up an effective means of communication that you mightn't have previously had the time, or the inclination, for. The benefit of mentoring is that it can help make staff aware of their personal weaknesses, while suggesting ways to work around them and turn them into strengths. Communication basically becomes more effective. Because you'll be spending time guiding your staff in their professional growth, you'll develop a great rapport with them. You'll support them, and they'll support you, which has to be good for your business.

23 Question: *What's it worth paying other people to do?*

Answer: *Only outsource skills that aren't strategic to your business.*

Outsourcing is one of those things that large organisations do every day. They pay other people to do the IT and the payroll. They outsource their new customer contact to call centres. They get someone else to organise their publicity. Small businesses, however, don't often buy into the concept. You often can't afford to pay other people to do things such as preparing your BAS, designing your website or helping you hire staff. But doing all this stuff yourself can come at a cost: the opportunity cost of you not working on your business. The smart thing to do, even if you're in the early stages of your business's growth, is to assess the specific tasks within your business and decide what you could possibly outsource one day and what you should definitely keep in-house. Look at the thought process as a big-picture planning opportunity; just one of the many you should be making time for every week.

Are the skills strategic?

First take a good look around your business: are you making the most of your skills and the resources of your team? Would you be better off paying for one of your employees to learn the skills you need than paying someone on the outside to do it? Keeping things in-house does have its advantages, according to Professor Ian Williamson from the Melbourne Business School. 'When you outsource knowledge-type activities, you create a tremendous reliability on your supplier that can then dictate your services to your clients', he says. His tip: look at every activity and ask yourself, is this one that should be part of your central strategy? If the answer is yes, it's part of your core business, so don't outsource it.

Should I learn it?

The more you outsource, the less likely it is that you and your team will ever be competent at certain tasks. While this may be fine in some areas of your business, in others it might leave you short when it comes to future capabilities. Williamson suggests asking yourself: is this particular task a competency that makes sense for you or your team to learn? Will this make the people in your organisation better? By outsourcing knowledge-type activities, you're not bolstering your own business's intellectual property. Usually, the more experience your business has in a range of tasks, the better off you'll be down the track.

What to keep in-house

This will all depend on your strengths and the strengths of your team members. Sales is possibly one of the only areas that you definitely should not outsource, suggests Williamson. He thinks it's also best to keep your recruiting in-house, so that you have control over who fits with your business's culture (see question 19). However, if you don't have time for the whole recruiting process (you just want to make your decision at the end), you can outsource your recruiting to an agency. Just make sure you have briefed them on who you are (your attitude to business), exactly what your business does and the type of person you think will fit into your team. As most standard outsourced recruiting companies work off a job description, it's up to you to get it right and brief them well.

How much risk?

One of the reasons businesses outsource duties is to mitigate their risk (see question 7 for the advisers you'll need the phone numbers of). You always need to have qualified financial reports, so it makes sense to have them done properly by a professional. Even entering data into your accounting package can be done haphazardly; this could cost your business when you do your quarterly BAS (remember question 11?). If you decide it could be wise to at least try outsourcing these things, make sure the person you pay to do the job is up to the task. Outsourcing is about entering into a relationship with the contractor, so find out all you can about them. Mitigating your own risk is a great reason to be fussy.

Who's accountable?

Paying people to do tasks for your business is one thing. Working out how you are going to hold them accountable can be another. 'Are you delegating or abdicating?' asks Kathryn Conder, partner of executive and business mentoring firm Carnegie Management Group. If you're not holding people accountable, you're abdicating. This can mean that your business could be held hostage by a contractor unless you have some controls in place. A watertight brief is essential. For example, restrict creative people to the parameters you put around a particular outsourced job. 'It's critical not to lose control by giving an adequate brief from the start', says Conder. This doesn't mean you need the same sorts of policies and procedures as bigger businesses. Just writing down some of the roles and responsibilities you need fulfilled, and talking it over with the outsourcer, can be a great way of holding them accountable.

Where do I look?

If you're going to outsource business functions, you want to be getting as much bang for your buck as you can. Look at the sort of expertise you don't have. If it's not worth your team learning, then look to a reputable company for solutions. Talk to other business owners you know who've used outside contractors. One such area of specialist knowledge is your graphic design and website development. Other areas are IT support and accountants (due to regulatory requirements). You also can think creatively about finding the right contractor. One firm Kathryn Conder knows was doing everything manually. They had their accountant help them set their systems up properly and then they got a second year uni student to do the inputting. 'The benefit was that as both went along they were learning', she says.

Measuring outsourcing success

A worldwide report from KPMG released in 2007, titled *Strategic evolution—A global survey on outsourcing today*, found that many businesses (mostly large ones) didn't quantify the benefits of outsourcing to their bottom line (42 per cent of outsourcing agreements were not formally measured). Learn from their oversight: always try to measure the business outcomes of anything you pay other people to do.

- *Innovation.* Has the outsourcer improved your service delivery or your processes?

- *Business alignment.* Has it been a cost benefit to your business?

- *Competitor performance.* Has outsourcing given you a competitive edge?

Measuring outsourcing success *(cont'd)*

▫ *Employee attitudes.* Did the outsourcer fit in terms of personality and ethos and did they work well with the rest of your team?

▫ *Productivity improvements.* Did outsourcing the task allow you time to work on building your business?

▫ *Operational performance measurements.* Is your staff satisfied with the service?

Source: KPMG International <www.kpmg.com.au>.

Part IV

Pump up the volume

Sales and marketing are the lifeblood of your business. In this part, you'll find out how to get up close and personal with your customers. The aim is to make your business stand out from the crowd. You'll also find information on some of the newest marketing opportunities and how you can use them to convert interest into sales.

To get the most out of this information, you'll need to devote some time to researching your market. What makes your customers, and potential customers, tick? What do they really want when it comes to your product or service offering? How can you reach them in the cheapest but most effective way? Understand this, and you'll be setting your business up for even greater success.

24

Question: *How do I develop a brand that will stand the test of time?*

Answer: *Make it 'unique' in some way.*

'A product is something that is made in a factory: a brand is something that is bought by customers. A product can be copied by a competitor: a brand is unique. A product can be quickly outdated: a successful brand is timeless.' So said advertising guru Stephen King back in the late 1960s. His words still ring true when it comes to developing a brand that can stand the test of time. Think about it in terms of your business. What is it about your brand that makes it unique? What sort of things do customers associate with your name, logo and positioning in the market? For Hungry Jack's, the burgers are better. For Avis, we try harder. These positioning statements have created an emotional response in their customers. Then the products deliver on their promise. In return, customers become loyal to these brands.

Defining your brand

It's a bit like the chicken and the egg conversation: which comes first? Do you define your brand first, or is it created through customers' experience of your product or service? 'The basic message of your brand has to be driven by your customers', says Michelle Gamble, founder and director of Marketing Angels. Think about what's distinctive about your product or service and why people buy your brand over your competition'. She says research is a critical part of finding this out: 'People measure customer satisfaction but not why they bought in the first place, and why they continue to buy. It's all about getting them to articulate your point of difference', she says. Then direct this back at them in every part of your marketing message.

Think it through

If you haven't thought about your brand thoroughly, how can you expect your customers to? 'I can't tell you how many times

I've seen business owners skimp on some of the most critical elements of presenting a successful brand', says Gamble. These elements include packaging, photography, printing, websites that are never updated and marketing emails sent to people who've never subscribed to receive them.

Yet every element is crucial when it comes to how you're perceived. The important thing, Gamble says, is to build consistency across all mediums of communication, and look for opportunities. According to the Sensis publication *Small Business, Big Opportunity* (you can access the book at <www.about.sensis.com.au/small_business>), companies that are able to manage their brands well can cover more than one market segment. Sensis says: 'For example, you might find generation Z don't recognise brands such as Microsoft and Sony, but they do know PlayStation and Xbox. This illustrates how both Sony and Microsoft are managing their brands at a generational level.'

Standing out from the crowd

You can still be in business without 'managing' your brand. You just won't do as well, particularly if you're working in a crowded market. To succeed, develop your unique selling proposition (USP) so you can stand out from the crowd. 'Look for that one flaw or missing element that all the other products in your category haven't cracked', Gamble advises on her blog at <www.marketingangels.com.au>. Once you find it, then find a solution so that you can be the one to deliver it to customers.

If you can crack that missing element, you'll know you've got something really special and you have something to hang your hat on, Gamble says. It can give your brand a story when you go to market. If told well, this story will bring your brand to life, motivating and influencing your customers along the way. Take the story of Diana Williams, the woman who created the Fernwood gym franchise. 'She knew she felt uncomfortable in normal gyms and asked her friends if they felt the same', says Gamble. A huge part of her success (in 2008 Fernwood was named joint winner of *BRW*'s most successful private business under $100 million) was knowing that there was a market there for her product. 'She tested the validity of the idea with her friends', says Gamble. The fact is, it doesn't have to be complicated, but most small businesses miss the opportunity to find out this information in the first place.

Action item: brand test

Try this quick exercise on your own brand. Think of a new tag line for your business: a catchy one-liner that instantly tells potential customers your unique selling proposition. Then take it through this brand test:

◻ How is it different to what you already have? Is it better? Why or why not?

◻ Ask everyone you can—friends, family and your staff. What do they think? What words come into their minds and how would they describe your offering to a friend?

◻ Does this translate to what you and your team do in your business every day?

◻ Finally, choose some loyal customers, and show your new slogan to them to find out what they think. Use all this information to hone your future marketing activities.

Communicating this difference

A lot of small businesses think that marketing is advertising. It's not. Gamble says marketing is about getting a message out about your brand, doing research and finding out what motivates your target market. First, find out what your customers want, and aim to deliver it. 'Then it's about promoting your message in the right places and tracking the results.' You can actually market your brand without spending a cent on advertising. To do this, she says, you have to work hard: you could set up networking events (see question 33 for some tips) and spend time improving your search engine optimisation (for more on this, see question 29). Capture any information people give you on how they perceive your brand. And don't waste the results. Instead, use your customer comments every chance you get, including on your future marketing material such as print ads, brochures and press releases, and in websites and blogs (for more online ideas, see question 30).

Regardless of whether your brand has been around for a while or you're developing a new one, you need firm ideas of why it's the best. Once you know, you'll be able to communicate this difference effectively throughout your business. Take the example of Fernwood Fitness as our test case: after 19 years of operation the brand now has 89 per cent unprompted recall of its brand name. The proof of its success is that other people endorse the brand. How would yours stack up?

25 Question: *Should I ever reinvent my marketing message?*

Answer: *Before you do anything, find out what your customers think.*

People's tastes change. It's up to you to know your customers, and how any changes in their buying behaviour translate into your business. Think of it as putting your finger on their purse pulse. If it's hot and thumping when they think of your brand offering, you're in a good place, and you need to keep it that way. If their reaction is fading out fast, either because they have gone cold on your idea or something better has come along, it's time to reinvigorate your message.

Start with the end in mind, says Michelle Gamble, founder and director of Marketing Angels <www.marketingangels.com.au>.

What is your goal for your business? 'Marketing has to be strategic in the sense that it has to link to what you want to do in your business', she says. Most small businesses look at marketing as a 'generally ad hoc activity'. They usually spot a market, and then put goods or services out there to see what works. What they forget about is taking a step back and creating brand awareness in the marketplace. 'Businesses that have done really well in good times, but not created any brand awareness, can find that their markets have dried up overnight', she adds. No-one but your current customers know about you, and when they stop purchasing, you have no fall-back. 'Hopefully, when small businesses are in this situation, they have some capital and can work out what potential new markets are out there', says Gamble. 'The worst thing they can do is do nothing.'

Spend the time

Effectively getting your brand message out there can actually be inexpensive, if you're smart and prepared to spend the time on it. Investigate email marketing, which is great if it's done well because it's an instant communication with your customers (see breakout box, p. 112). Gamble also suggests developing a blog, where you can write about your business (see more on how to do this in question 30). Then there's the mainstream media, where you can develop a story for newspapers and radio (if that's what your customers are reading and listening to). 'Even something as simple as a regular phone call to a customer every two to three months gives you the opportunity to see how you're delivering on your promise', says Gamble.

Another tool is to develop customer surveys. Or you could offer customers networking opportunities so that you can thank them, but also use the event to get more information out of them (check question 33 for networking tips). While all these things need your time, it's the one thing that you, as a small business owner, can invest in, particularly if you don't have stacks of money to spend on sophisticated marketing strategies.

What makes a good marketing email?

Emails go straight to customers' computers: treat them as you would any other serious marketing opportunity. Michelle Gamble has these tips on getting the best results from marketing emails:

- Have a goal: are you doing it to acquire customers or retain them? Acquisition emails are email campaigns. Their purpose is to get the customer to take action, such as buying a product, visiting a store or entering a competition. Retention emails are email newsletters, which develop a relationship to drive loyalty, referrals and purchasing in the long term. There's no hard sell. 'I suggest if you want to do both, do it in separate emails so you can maximise your opportunity to achieve your goal', says Gamble.

- Have a list: make sure the people on your database want to receive emails, and have an unsubscribe link in all your emails. 'Have a double-opt-in process for anyone who subscribes so that they confirm that they want to get your email', adds Gamble. While it might shrink your list, it's now getting to people who want it.

- Get it opened: Gamble says that the way to get your email opened 'is to make sure that the receiver recognises the sender'. Think about who it will be from (you or your company), and also personalise the subject line.

- Get it read: short and sweet is the best message. Use bold type and links to attract their attention. And try to get your whole message into the first five lines so that the viewer doesn't have to scroll down to see what you're about. 'Keep the full story on your website and link to it from the newsletter', says Gamble.

▢ Test and tweak: use different parts of your email list to test different subject lines, content and offers. This will help you 'see what works best and maximise your effectiveness', says Gamble.

▢ The timing: send emails out early in the week. She says that the highest email open rates occur on a Monday, with the lowest on a Friday.

Target the action

Of course, exactly what you do will depend on where your business is at in its life cycle, and what your plan is for the business. Gamble says that when you're starting up a small business, it's about getting the brand right, and developing consistency and a great story from day one. 'Focus on what's going to interest the market', she says. 'Do your research and find out what the appetite is like for your product.' In the growth stage of your business, you should stay on top of things by measuring your marketing activity. 'Where are you getting your leads from?' she asks. 'How much money are you budgeting for marketing?'

In the plateau phase of a business's life cycle, Gamble recommends looking at innovation. 'It might pay you to go back and look at the trends in your industry, and find out where the growth markets are', she says. Is it time to invest money in new products which you know will reinvigorate your brand? In the crisis stage, when a customer's reaction to your business is flat-lining, it's important that you try not to panic. Focus on getting your marketing to shout about your brand. That's where online marketing and referral relationships come into their own because they can quickly and effectively get vital messages out to your customers. No matter where your business falls in terms of its life cycle, the key is to continually monitor your market.

Hot on their trail

'If you're a retail or consumer business, your point of sale system can give you an invaluable amount of information on your customer', says Gamble. If your point of sale (POS) system isn't giving you this information, you should look at changing to one that will track where customers are from, how much each customer spends and what they buy. Both MYOB and QuickBooks have POS integration systems. She also thinks that every small business should have a good website, 'not just a page with your brand on it, but something you drive your customers to for more information and special offers'. Then, by using free tools such as Google Analytics, you can capture information on your customers and what they're interested in. If your website isn't exciting them, you can change things easily, without having to spend too much (for more on this go to question 29).

If you're a business-to-business enterprise, Gamble recommends a lot of direct marketing and selling through established networks. 'A good database and tracking system are essential', she says. 'You can pull reports, from tracking keywords on your website right through to the sale.' Invest in a customer relationship management (CRM) system and database set-up so that you can capture information about your customers and where they go on your website. There are many different types of CRM systems on the market. Before you buy, it helps to know what you need: there's no point spending thousands of dollars on a fancy CRM system if you're only going to utilise the basic features. For a great run-down on what some of the best ones offer, check out the article 'The Best CRM Suite is...' on the ZDNet Australia website (<www.zdnet.com.au>; type 'CRM suite' into the site search).

ZDNet road-tested six CRM products and rated Salesforce.com CRM as the best solution for small businesses.

The best tracking systems in the world aren't worth looking at until *you* totally understand your brand essence. Why did you set up your business in the first place? Is the core of your business about trust? Or is it about fun? And is this what appeals to your target market? Thinking this through will give you some important marketing hooks. By defining the personality of your brand, you can then make it part of every piece of internal and external communication that comes out of your office. Consistency is the key.

26 Question: *What's the best way to look big without letting on that I'm a small fry?*

Answer: *Believe in being professional in everything you do.*

Large companies pitch themselves as professional set-ups. Their offices look slick. Their people walk the walk. Every contact with customers, either on the phone or via letters or email, has a unified message. Cut to small business. You and your team get along well with people and you're mostly self-taught when it comes to delivering good customer service. Your marketing material — business cards, letterhead and flyers — were designed by a friend when you first set up (or you might have done them yourself). Your website is still a work in progress. However, what you do have is a monster-sized desire to make your product or service succeed. You are innovative and creative. If you can transfer some of those qualities into every part of your business, you'll never have to worry about looking like a small fry.

Create a culture

Look on the inside. That's what mega company Hewlett Packard did when it first set up in 1939. Founders Dave Packard and Bill Hewlett were uni students working out of a garage next to Packard's rented home (check out the garage at <www. hp.com/hpinfo/abouthp/histnfacts/>). They invented the audio oscillator: a unique product which Walt Disney Studios bought eight of to test on the sound system for the movie *Fantasia*. However, the emphasis for Dave and Bill wasn't only on innovative products. They set out to create a vibrant workplace to rival their biggest competitors. In their first year of operation they paid staff Christmas bonuses and made their first corporate donation (US$5 to local charities). They devel-oped a strong corporate identity that was inclusive from day one. And successful. The valuable lesson for your small business is that making your staff feel valuable counts for something. So don't underestimate the power in the perception that your business is bigger than the jobs your people do every day.

Smoke and mirrors

Once you've looked at your internal culture, think about your business from your customers' perspective. What do *they* want from you? While an address of 2 Smith St, Upper Suburbia is code for small, this can work in your favour if your business is focused on local clientele. They like the fact that you're just around the corner. However, if you're trying to compete statewide, nationally or globally, it's probably time to change your postal address if you don't want to be considered small fry. And don't settle for the local post office. Have a look at what it would cost you to get a post office box at your city GPO. Prices for GPO post boxes vary between cities, so check out <www.auspost.com.au> or call your nearest Australia Post outlet for prices and details. Your mail can then be redirected to your local post office, business or home address. While this will cost you, it gives you the ability to look like you're a big-city player, and with this comes big-end-of-town cred with customers who prefer to deal with larger companies.

Mastering a marketing plan

Large companies always know where they're going with their marketing. They never fly blind. And neither should you. So spend the time and put together a marketing plan for your business. It doesn't have to be complicated. But when you're putting it together, you should be systematic, clear about why you're doing it, and know how you're going to measure the results. According to the Australian Government's site <www.business.gov.au> (which offers several free marketing plan templates), it pays to think about the following basic elements:

- analysis of your current market (who is or will be your customer, and everything you know about them and their purchasing habits; plus who are your competitors)

- your business objectives (what do you want to achieve?)

- key strategies (how you're going to get there)

- steps to achieving your objectives (which comes first, the chicken or the egg?)

- proposed budget (define how much you're prepared to spend)

- timing (when's the best moment to strike?).

Source: <www.business.gov.au>.

Free to phone

As with your address, having a local business phone number is fine if you're dealing locally. But if your customers are coming from far and wide, it's a great idea to invest in a toll-free phone number. The benefit of these is that they take your business location out of the equation. There are a range of toll-free services with different telcos: Telstra, for example, offers Freecall 1800, Priority One3, Priority 1300 and International Freecall. For most of these products your customers pay either nothing or a 'flat fee' (similar to a local call charge) to call you. Your business picks up the bill for the call. While it can be a great way to make customers think your help desk is substantial, it pays to check what each service offers and how much they'll cost you. Visit your local phone provider's website or Telstra at <www.telstrabusiness.com/business> (click on '1300 numbers' then 'Inbound Calling Services').

Answer that, will you?

If you're in start-up mode and working out of a home office, consider having a dedicated phone line for your business. That way, you'll always know it's a work call, and you can answer it professionally, every time. Then look at your answering machine. Does your message sound like a business you'd want to buy something from? If it doesn't, change it quickly. Do you even need an answering machine, or are you getting enough calls to warrant a voicemail service? If you opt for a voicemail service, put a professional business message on the line, rather than the home messaging service message which will make your customers think you're a small operation. Get one of your staff (preferably someone of the opposite sex to you) to create a professional-sounding voicemail message. If you don't have any staff, ask a friend to do you this favour.

What you see is what you get

You know that your communication with customers and suppliers has to be professional if you want to play with the big boys. But often small business lets itself down in the detail. Consider how your mail goes out from your office. Do you handwrite labels on parcels and envelopes? This smacks of small to customers and suppliers. Maybe you could get someone in your office to design and print out professional-looking labels. Or pay someone else to do it for you. Then, every envelope and parcel that leaves your office will look professional. And make it look consistent with your other marketing bits, such as your business cards. Plan the image you want to portray, what you're going to say, and how you're going to say it. This is all part of your marketing plan, which you should have (see the breakout box, p. 117, for tips on mastering your marketing plan if you haven't already put one together). Do the office paraphernalia well, and show that you mean business.

Take it online

Email addresses and websites are now just like phones and answering services: everyone has them, but not everyone uses them well. How many business email addresses do you see with their internet service provider (ISP) as part of their address: for example, yourbusiness@bigpond.com.au? Put your consumer hat on: these addresses send out the I've-just-set-up vibe. But email can become such a big part of how you do business, so it pays to lift your game. All you have to do is register for a domain name of your business. This secures your business's very own spot on the internet (your email address will be you@yourbusiness.com.au), and gives you a professional presence when you start using online marketing tools (more on that in question 30).

You can register your domain name yourself by going to the official domain name registration organisation in Australia: .au Domain Administration Ltd <www.auda.org.au>. Before you do, check that the domain name you want is actually available (someone may have already registered the domain name you want, which is unlucky as it's a first-come, first-served process). Go to the Australian Registry site <www.ausregistry.com.au> or phone it on (03) 9866 1970. If you register your domain name yourself you'll pay about $150 for two years' registration. If your ISP or website host registers it for you, expect to pay about $200. But it's worth it. Every time someone types you an email from now on, they'll be thinking about your business. It's called getting mileage out of your marketing.

Action item: don't forget your domain name

The Australian Government's e-business guide suggests you ask yourself the following questions when looking at registering your own domain name:

- Does the domain name support the branding of your organisation?

- Would your target audience guess the domain name and email address?

- Do the domain name and email address stand on their own and make sense?

- Is the domain name or email address too long, awkward to type or repeat verbally to people?

- Can the name be confused with an existing popular domain name?

Source: Department of Broadband, Communications and the Digital Economy's e-business guide at <www.e-businessguide.gov.au/understanding/start/email>.

---

27 **Question:** *How do I do market research that means something?*

Answer: *First work out what you want to know.*

Market research is all about getting answers. Does a particular group of people need a particular product or service? Would they pay money for it? How much would they pay? For start-up businesses, asking these questions is vital. Otherwise, how do you know there's a market for your brilliant idea? And what size it is? Doing some basic market research can reduce your risk because you'll go into the business with your eyes wide open. For existing small businesses, market research is about keeping your eyes open, and maintaining your competitive edge. How else will you know if your customers' purchasing habits are about to change, until it's too late and your product or service drops off their radar? How do you find out if your product or service is still giving customers or clients exactly what they want?

It's not enough to have great ideas. If you're going to have a sustainable and profitable small business, you need to know what excites your purchasers. It doesn't have to be a complex investigation. But it should be relevant, accurate and objective, according to Smart Skills, an online initiative of Queensland's Department of Tourism, Regional Development and Industry (its online tutorials on marketing and promotions are definitely worth a look; go to <www.sdi.qld.gov.au/virtual> and click on 'Marketing and promotions').

The site suggests starting your market research quest with your external environment: 'factors you can't control', such as any compliance issues in your industry or downturns in the broader economy. For example, if you're a builder you'll want to know what sorts of restrictions are placed on developments by your local council. These could significantly affect your future business. Then you should look at internal factors: 'factors you can control', such as your employees and your ongoing investment. Next is to collect detailed information about your customers. Think of it in terms of who they are, where they are, what they need and what they want. Finally, look at your competitor profile by putting together 'detailed information about your existing and possible future competitors', such as their market coverage, strengths and strategies.

By making these sorts of lists, you'll realise the factors that are within your control and those you have no control over. Being aware of these external factors, and possibly planning around them, will help build your business on firm footings. If the earth moves beneath you, you'll have contingencies in place to withstand the changes. The best sources of market information are the Australian Bureau of Statistics <www.abs. gov.au>, local councils if your business is within a particular geographical location, industry-specific government agencies and local media (newspapers and TV and radio reports). There's also a huge amount of information online regarding different groups of people. Just make sure you hit reputable sites in your hunt for information (state and federal government sites, libraries and universities are good places to start).

Market research for start-ups

If you're starting a small business, the Tasmanian Government suggests you try to find out the answers to the following questions:

- What are the long-term trends that will affect my business?

- How much business can I expect if I open at a certain location?

- Will people purchase my products or services?

- Who are my competitors?

- What range of products or services do my competitors offer?

- What level of sales do my competitors generate?

- Who are my customers likely to be?

- What types of products or services do my prospective customers want?

- What types of products or services do my prospective customers not want?

- What type of advertising will attract customers to my business?

Source: *Researching Your Market*, Department of Economic Development, Tourism and the Arts—Tasmanian Government.

What's it cost?

You don't have to pay a market research company to get meaningful market research results: you can do it yourself for free. You just have to be prepared to spend the time. According to the Queensland Department of Tourism, Regional Development and Industry, there are two types of research you can do: desk research, which are the things you can find out sitting at your desk (by reading books, journals, reports and on the internet); and field research, which is actually getting out there and having a look at customer habits, conducting surveys and asking people what they think.

There is also a less formal type of market research: asking your friends. While it can be useful asking friends what they think (the most useful ones will be friends who fit your customer profile), you should be prepared for their honest opinions (good and bad). Then it's worth going further afield in your research to validate their opinions. Unless, of course, you only want to sell to your friends!

Another free and fast research tool is the internet, particularly chatrooms. They are a great place to find a group of people you think might be in the market for your product (for ways to get into chatrooms and other types of social media, go to question 30). Connect with people and ask what they think. Again, always be ready for some pretty honest feedback from strangers. Tapping in to online forums used by your target market also can give you a real feel for how and why they purchase certain things over others. And this is one of the things you definitely want to find out.

What you get out of it

How can you develop a profitable relationship with a market of people if you don't know where and who they are? The idea of spending the time doing market research is that it gives you the chance to find out. Are you missing huge segments of potential purchasers? Should you rethink a business offering because it doesn't meet your market's needs or wants?

Market research for existing enterprises

You get different things out of market research if you're already operating a business. For a start, you have existing customers. The Tasmanian Government has come up with these questions for you:

- Who is my advertising directed at? Is it reaching them?
- Is there a change in my customers' spending habits?
- Have my competitors made any recent changes?
- What services should I offer my customers?
- Should I be offering more than I offer now?
- Should I vary my trading hours?
- Should I establish another outlet?
- What changes have occurred in the market?
- What scope exists to increase my prices?

Source: *Researching Your Market*, Department of Economic Development, Tourism and the Arts—Tasmanian Government.

Once you have a whole heap of facts together, you'll be in a better position to work out if your business can actually deliver. Will you be competitive with existing or new players? Do you have the capital to get it going, and keep your business ramped up? And do you, or the people you're employing, have the skills to make it all work? As it states in the marketing tutorial from Smart Skills, unless you're 100 per cent confident your answer to all these questions is a resounding yes, then you should rethink your business idea. Think of it as your Muhammad Ali moment: focus on what's moving in front of you, and then deliver a knockout punch that will make you heaps of money.

28 Question: *How do I find new customers?*

Answer: *Using traditional marketing tools can still snare you customers.*

Who are your customers? Successful small businesses know the answer to this question. Intimately. They spend a lot of time finding out everything they can about their clients: from their purchasing habits to how old they are, what they do professionally, their income levels and their marital status. To get new customers, you need to first understand who your existing customers are and how they perceive your product or service, says Michelle Gamble, director of Marketing Angels. So ask them. You might run a competition to find out what makes your customers tick. Or email them a survey. If your business is just starting out, Gamble suggests keeping it simple by asking the opinion of friends and family who fit the profile of who you are selling to. You could also try to find out what your competitors' customers like or don't like.

Once you have this information, you'll be able to be more strategic in your search for new customers. You'll understand what's going to attract them to your business and entice them to buy. Then you'll be able to make an informed decision on which of the following traditional marketing tools will reach your target market and work best for your business. (For information on technology-based marketing opportunities, such as an online presence, and social media, such as Twitter and Facebook, see questions 29 and 30.)

Be the expert

You know your business speciality better than anyone. But have you ever thought about setting yourself up in the local media as an expert that people go to for answers? For example, if your business is hairdressing, why not start a style spot column that you put together every week? Or an architect: you could give local readers or listeners the latest information in energy-saving renovation ideas for their houses. To be a well-informed font of knowledge gives you credibility in the broader community. And when people know of you, and feel they can trust you, they will be more likely to purchase from you.

Try to give local media the heads-up about any newsworthy developments in your field. Type up a press release and email or fax it to local media outlets. You'll be surprised how much free coverage you'll get if your story is worthwhile. If you don't think you have the expertise to put together a press release, it might be worthwhile talking to a public relations consultant to see what they can do for you (the Public Relations Institute of Australia has a list of PR consultants in your state at <www.pria.com.au/consultant>).

Partner up

You've done the research and know your market. You found out things like the kinds of cars they drive and where they go out for dinner. But where else do they shop? By identifying some other businesses your customers (or potentials) also patronise, you might be able to cross-sell your services with this business. In marketing terms, these are called channel partners. For example, if you're selling machinery to farmers, where do the farmers go to buy their fertiliser? Even their boots? If you're an accountant, where do your potential clients go for dinner? Pinpoint the businesses who deal with similar customers to you and try going to them with a proposal. Can you offer their existing customers a discount or a special offer? It has to be good enough to make it a win–win for your channel partner. Agree to share leads as you move forward: then you can both reap the rewards.

Customer referrals

People trust the opinions of others. So whether you have one customer or thousands, their recommendation can be pure gold to people who haven't heard of you before. First find out why they buy from you. Ask why they sometimes don't purchase your products. Then give them rewards for their loyalty. It could be a discount on a future purchase. Or a small gift. Or information that no-one else gets. If you can make them feel like they're an important part of your business, and they have a good experience, they'll most probably refer someone they know to experience your product or service, too. And if they do, thank them. It might come at a small cost to you, but calculate what it's worth if they bring you new customers.

Creating a buzz

Publicity stunts can draw new customers to your business like bees to a honey pot. They get existing and potential customers talking. They attract media attention. Big companies pay big money for celebrity endorsements of their products, but publicity stunts don't have to cost a lot of money. For example, one owner of a city coffee business set out to fill the world's biggest coffee cup outside her store. Fashion outlets have used live mannequins. The idea is to stop your target market in their tracks. Once you've done this, the next step is to work out how to get them to buy from you or use your services. Creating a buzz around your business will attract people to it. The question is, can you convert their interest into a sale? (For advice on how to do this, see question 32.)

Direct to their door

There are a couple of other traditional ways to attract new customers: direct mail campaigns and buying a list or database of prospective names. Australia Post, for example, offers direct mail services that get information about your business into people's hands (for information and costs on its Direct Mail Toolkit, go to <www.auspostbusiness.com.au> and click on 'Marketing Your Business'). The best tip if you're considering using any direct mail service is to track your response rate, and measure if it's worked. Use a targeted offer that new customers (or existing ones) can redeem if they call your business or go into your store (you can use specific codes for different areas of the country).

You also can buy a list of customers in your target market from a database (Australia Post offers this service too). Just don't waste your money on direct mail or database campaigns that just talk about your business. Create an emotional response in your message. Give new customers a call to action. Kristina Mills of Words That Sell <www.wordsthatsell.com.au> says it pays to be a bit creative when it comes to the email subject lines you use: for example 'Are you calling in today?'; 'This is the key to "having it all"'; 'Will it work for me?'; 'What is your "Money Attractor" IQ?' Then be ready for your customers when they come.

Action item: moving messages

Do you have your business name and website emblazoned on your car? In most cases it's really hard to measure the effectiveness of the tactic. Sure, potential customers can see your name and phone number, or website address, on your car, but they may have no idea what your business offers, and why they should be interested. Here are some ways to improve your results:

□ Think strategically about what you put on your car.

□ Give passersby and other motorists a quick idea of what you're offering, and why they need your product or service.

- Make them an offer in the ad which they can think about as they're stuck in traffic. For example, if you're a dentist, it could be: Free toothpaste. Get yours at Friendly Dentists (followed by your website).

- If you're going to spend the money on having your car spray painted to market your business, use it well!

29 Question: *What about online?*

Answer: *Consider your website as the first stage of your online strategy.*

Having an online presence is now nearly as necessary for small business as a phone. For many, it has even more potential to boost business, and create success. Just look at what it did for Barack Obama during his run for the US presidency. He used the internet to invigorate a whole generation of nonvoters to go out and make their vote count. So if Barack Obama could harness the power of the medium to get him into the White House as the first black American president, surely there are some amazing opportunities out there for your small business.

In the past, online activity has been the domain of big business. Small business has been slower to catch on. According to an Australian Bureau of Statistics survey in 2007, 95 per cent of businesses with 200 or more employees had a web presence (of these, 69.1 per cent placed orders via the web, and 25.9 per cent received orders online). In businesses with between five and 19 employees, 44.3 per cent had a web presence (of these, 48.4 per cent placed orders via the internet and 29.1 per cent received orders online), and of businesses with up to four employees, 24 per cent had a web presence (of these, 34.3 per cent placed orders via the web and 20 per cent received orders online).

Businesses that don't get with the program could be seriously disadvantaged in the future as even more people start shopping online. 'A website represents a fantastic opportunity to create a good first impression, turn cold leads into sales and potentially building operational gains leading to real return on investment', says Michelle Gamble, director of Marketing Angels.

Identify your goals

Don't set and forget a website like you would other marketing paraphernalia, such as business cards or stationery. 'If you don't spend time on it and do it properly, it's a bit like having the TV turned on with the sound turned down', adds Gamble. Before you contemplate how your website looks, there are a heap of things to consider. We'll cover a few here, but it also will be worthwhile searching around for information yourself. Go to the web industry's professional associations, such as the Web Industry Association (<www.webindustry. asn.au>) and the Web Industry Professionals Association (<http://wipa.org.au/>).

First off, designer Sharri Boucher of Jakiti Design <www. jakitidesign.com> suggests you think about: do you want to sell products or not? Do you want to process credit cards instantly? Do you want to send newsletters to your customers? Do you want to be able to update the site yourself? Michelle Gamble says you also need to think about whether or not you want to capture leads and build your database from visitors to your website. Boucher adds: 'Consider where you want to be in five years' time and try and make sure that the website will grow with you'.

DIY or use a designer?

You can design your own basic website. However, to do this well (so that you achieve a professional-looking site), it will pay to do a fair bit of homework. You have to get it right: a dodgy-looking site is a death knell to any business. Two popular build-your-own-website sites are <www.homestead. com> and <www.chilliwebsites.com>. Find out if the capabilities of the web designs that are provided as templates match your online objectives. If you want a website that's either more responsive to your business (with a structured customer relationship management system so you can update the content yourself whenever you want) or a site with bells and whistles and a secure e-commerce solution, you might be better off contacting a web designer (either through the web associations listed previously or the *Yellow Pages*). Remember, leave the brain surgery to the brain surgeons!

What to ask

Boucher says you should be armed with a stack of questions for any prospective web designer. Don't hold back. What is their experience, education and training and are they accredited by the web industry associations? Get examples of their work and testimonials from previous clients. If it's a larger web design company you're looking at, who will be working on your account and who will own the intellectual property once your site is designed? Do they customise designs or use templates (this, and whether or not you have a CMS on your site, will influence the cost) and are there any bandwidth and space limitations on their designs?

What does a website cost?

There are many different costs that need to be factored in to your website design decision, according to designer Sharri Boucher. Here's the shopping list she suggests you take to a web design candidate:

What does a website cost? *(cont'd)*

▫ *Web design.* Does the cost cover the entire site, or just the design? Do you require a logo? Do you require stock photos? Do you require a copywriter? Which company will be your web host—the physical location of your website? What's their annual fee?

▫ *Domain name registration.* This is usually a 48-month registration. Do you want multiple domain names to help bring traffic to your site. Do you want a .com or .com.au URL? Do you want .net, .biz or other extensions? What about a Content Management System—do you need one?

▫ *E-commerce systems.* These have additional costs such as: SSL (Secure Socket Layer protocol) Certificates to encrypt information on your site; connectivity to bank costs; the costs on individual transactions; PayPal connectivity (usually a percentage on each transaction, with extra charges for currency conversions).

▫ *Online advertising capabilities.* Will the designer company submit your website to search engines (usually a one-off cost)? Will they sign you up with Google Adwords (see question 31 for more on this) and get your banner ads on other larger, well-known websites?

▫ *Miscellaneous costs.* These should be confirmed before design and development commences, and include: product information upload; price per page costs; specialised image costs.

How long does it take?

Customised sites take longer than ones designed from existing templates. 'Customised sites allow you to design the site around your business', says Boucher. Ready-made templates are a quick way to get your business online: if you give a designer prepared content and design ideas, your site can be up in a few days. More complicated websites, such as elaborately designed e-commerce sites, can take months. To save time and money, Boucher suggests having your web design ideas ready. Spend time looking around at other websites and decide on what elements (such as colour, layout and navigation systems) you like or dislike. Cut out things from magazines. Collect paint colour chips from hardware stores of colour combinations you like and bring them along to the meeting. 'This all helps the designer to understand the style you want for your business', she adds.

The power of the search

Once it's designed, the aim of the game is for your site to be ranked as highly as possible when people search for information over the internet. This is known as search engine optimisation (SEO). 'Keep in mind that there is often a trade-off between beautiful, graphically represented sites and search engine rankings', says Michelle Gamble. 'This is because of the way Google, for example, searches for sites with relevant content.'

Google and other search engines basically trawl the world wide web for information on particular search words or topics, known as keywords. Your aim is to have your business site ranked at number one on the first page of a Google search for your primary keyword or keywords (to find out how, see the 'Action item: boosting your Google ranking'). Work hard at optimising your appeal in search engine terms, and you'll give your business the best chance to get even more business.

Action item: boosting your Google ranking

The Australian Web Industry Association offers some great tips for website owners on how you can boost your Google ranking and what to consider when it comes to search engine optimisation. Some of the information relates to getting professional help in this area, but it also gives you a great overview of the concept. Go to <www.webindustry.asn.au>, click on the 'documents' link and then the PDF 'Search Engine Optimisation—Choosing the Right Provider'.

30 **Question:** *Can internet fads such as Twitter and Facebook make me money?*

Answer: *Social media 'fads' are starting to have a positive impact on business.*

If marketing is all about getting your message out and building relationships, then you really can't afford to ignore the online phenomenon known as social media. It's Stage Two of your online plan. While it used to be great if your business simply had a website (if you don't have one yet, go straight back to question 29), in the future you're going to need more. You're going to need a website *and* a vibrant online presence, so that you're actively engaging with customers and potential clients. The social media phenomenon isn't about pushing your product. It's all about using technology to create conversations with your existing and potential customers. If you do it right, it's a veritable Aladdin's Cave of opportunities.

What is social media?

When people talk about social media (and every marketing expert is), they're referring to an ever-growing array of web-based tools to help people create online networks. These tools include blogs (where you publish or 'post' your own online content, separately from your website if you want) and RSS feeds (which stands for Rich Site Summary or Really Simple Syndication: it keeps you up to date with any new content from your favourite websites and blogs). Then there are social networks (including Facebook, MySpace and LinkedIn) and 'microblogs' such as Twitter (where you post a message using no more than 140 characters to tell your network what you're doing 'right now'). If this all sounds like Swahili to you, don't panic. There are whole books being written about social media. Basically, it's a brave new world that digital technology coach John Jantsch, of Duct Tape Marketing, says has already transformed the way businesses market themselves.

'If you studied marketing in the textbook world, you likely covered the 4 Ps of marketing', he says. 'You simply created a Product, figured out how to Price it, got it Placed in the market, and Promoted the heck out it.' In his e-book *Let's Talk: social media for small business* (you can download it for free from <www.ducttapemarketing.com>), he says that the new marketing checklist involves the '4 Cs'. This involves having 'relevant, education-based, and perhaps user-generated Content that is filtered, aggregated, and delivered in a Context that makes it useful for people who are starving to make Connections with people, products, and brands they can build a Community around'.

Like anything new, until you try it, it's hard to get your head around how it really works. 'It's how business is being done', agrees Michelle Gamble, founder of Marketing Angels. She says that, in some ways, getting active online can take away some of the scariness of getting your message out there. 'It's quick, it's targeted, it's instantly measurable, and it's free', she adds. It's also here to stay. So you may as well at least understand how the technology works. Once you see what the buzz is all about, you might even start using it to boost your business.

Who's getting involved

Locally focused small businesses can benefit just as much from using online social media tools as global enterprises are starting to. 'Facebook and Twitter are having a huge impact', says Gamble. 'These networks are a great way of disseminating information really quickly.'

Small Business Victoria has formed its own Facebook group to 'network and share information' (check out the 'I am a business owner in Victoria, Australia' Facebook group at <www.facebook.com>). And Gamble tells the story of a coffee shop in the US that used Twitter to take orders from clients, boosting its client numbers in the process (read about the success yourself via <www.marketingangels.com.au>).

Business opportunities and success stories are happening every day online because customers are engaging with the technology (check out Mumu Grill's story below). They are telling their friends about the great information they're finding. Valuable word-of-mouth referrals are flooding in to businesses like yours without much effort from you and no cost (other than the time it takes you to type).

Success story

Mumu Grill <www.mumugrill.com.au>, a steakhouse in Crows Nest, Sydney, has had phenomenal business success since its launch in 2008. And restaurant owner Craig Macindoe attributes much of it to his use of Facebook, Twitter and blogging. 'About 12 months ago I decided I needed to understand how the new media worked and how it could work for my business, so I got myself on Facebook', he says. Then he formed a Facebook group called Mumu Grill, where people who weren't his friends could join in the conversation. 'I invited people to comment on my posts and blogs, which could be about anything, from what's good at the markets on Wednesday mornings to recipes I'm using. I posted other people's feedback and links to other food sites and blogs and it didn't take long before more and more people engaged in what was going on at Mumu Grill', he says.

Then Macindoe started hosting business networking events and wine dinners at his steakhouse. 'I invited people who were following me on Twitter (he now has 2500 followers) to the events. Initially there wasn't much of a response, but then I started having 20 to 30 people coming along. To the most recent one, I had 95 people: the restaurant was absolutely full.'

He spends about five hours each week using social media, which includes updating his Facebook page with photos or news from the restaurant, putting out four or five tweets and quickly checking Twitter each time he goes on his computer. He also writes two or three new blogs a month (you can check them out through the Mumu website), depending on what he's been doing and what he thinks people will be interested in.

'The return on investment (for his time) has been astronomical', he says. 'For example, I have just started doing live bookings online, and in two weeks over 200 people have made reservations. I did a search of where the leads for the bookings have come from (using a tool similar to Google Analytics). They are all from people naturally going to our website because they have heard of us through other online links, or they have seen us on Twitter. I would say we're up 30 to 40 per cent on last year, and at least half of that is due to social media.'

How you can start

Jantsch rates blogs as the best place to launch into the social media universe. Leave Twitter, Facebook and LinkedIn until you know a bit more about how it works. Start by reading as many blogs as you can. To find them, simply type the words 'small business blogs' into a Google search. If you've heard about any blogs written by others in your industry, or experts you respect, check them out. You'll soon get a feel for what people write online. Then you should have a go at adding your comments to some of the blogs you like. 'This is an important part of online networking and may help get your blog noticed down the road', says Jantsch.

After a couple of weeks of investigations, you'll be ready to launch your own blog. This involves installing free blog software on to your computer (you'll find lots of this software online: WordPress <www.wordpress.org> and TypePad <www.typepad.com> are easy ones to understand). Then it's a matter of creating your own content (known as a post). You really can write about anything, and it can be as long or short as you like. For business blogs, however, it's a good idea to keep the content relevant to your business interest. Maybe blog about the latest news from your industry, any press you've had, how the development of a new product is going, or some facts you think your customers might find interesting too. It all helps you get connected and creates a buzz around your business.

A dynamic strategy

The new breed of online business content is dynamic, changing weekly, if not daily. So you do have to be constantly monitoring it, checking for feedback and adding new posts to your blog. Gamble says it's time well spent because your blog can become a credible platform for dialogue with your customers. Her advice is for small businesses to have a crack at all the different types of social media. 'And remember that what you give in to this medium, you will get back', she adds.

John Jantsch says you don't have to start your social media experience on your own: 'Creating a blog and then recruiting a group of authors who have strong strategic referral partner potential is a killer local marketing idea', he says. For example, he thinks a plumber, electrician, lawn-mowing service and heating and cooling company could make a great home tips blogging team: 'That group would dominate the local home repair (online) searches that have become the norm for homeowners frustrated with trying to find good help.' Being up on the first page of a Google search just because you've got a dynamic blog is a strategic business move. 'This group could eventually start putting together all-day workshops and seminars based on the multiauthor blog format, much like a magazine', adds Jantsch. All power!

Action item: understanding the idea

If you're still not sold on the whole idea of social media, there's an interesting, and free, online video that explains the concept of information sharing by comparing it to ice-cream. Go to the Social Media in Plain English site at <www.commoncraft.com/socialmedia>. It'll take less than four minutes to have the light turned on in your head.

31

Question: *I spend so much on advertising, so where are the results?*

Answer: *To get results you really need to track your every move.*

The whole idea of advertising is that it brings you business. Makes you money. Grows your reputation and your customer base. But it's also much more. Every advertisement is like a window into the soul of your business. It can reveal what you're about, how professional you are and how you treat your customers. Do you view them as intelligent beings who know what they want? Or do you assume that just because they're reading, watching or listening to an ad, they'll happily buy into any old proposition you put to them? If you've ever placed an ad in print, online or on TV or radio, you might already know what worked and what didn't. That's assuming you actually put in some strategies to measure the results. However, most businesses don't.

Only about half of all advertising efforts get results (such as phone enquiries, leads and ultimately sales). It's just that most small businesses don't know which half. Plus, you may only advertise when you need results fast: a quick fix to a downturn or stock issues. Then when the ad doesn't work, it's the ad's fault. 'An advertisement can generate many phone calls, but if they are the wrong callers, it won't generate sales, only cost you time and lost opportunity while you take the calls', states a publication called *Small Business, Big Opportunity* produced by leading Australian information provider Sensis (check out a full version of the book at the Sensis website <www.about.sensis.com.au/small_business>).[1] To get the right callers, what you first need to do is identify your 'ideal customer', and get inside their head. Once you understand who they are and why they buy, then you can focus on the message and the medium you'll use to target them. And try not to be desperate for results.

First, identify your customer

To find out who your 'ideal customer' is, *Small Business, Big Opportunity* suggests asking questions such as: What do they read? What websites do they visit? What associations are they members of? Otherwise, how else are you going to know where to place your ads? If your business is aimed at lots of

---

[1] Sensis Pty Ltd ABN 30 007 423 912 Copyright 2009.

different people, choose which groups of customers you want to reach out to every time you advertise. Then try to work out the language they're likely to respond to, the types of things they want to hear, and why. Including all this in your ads will get a better response.

Know what you want to say

When you know who you're communicating to in an ad, Sensis recommends you concentrate on 'the essence' of what you're going to say to them. This shouldn't be any more than a couple of sentences. Advertising experts call it the 'elevator pitch'. It's where a person needs to have understood your message in the time it takes them to get in an elevator or lift and get to their floor. What would you say to them to get them interested in your product or service if you had such a short time? This is all about putting yourself in your customers' shoes. Why should they buy your product or service? What's in it for them?

Know what you can say

In 2007 there were 2602 complaints about ads, according to the Advertising Standards Bureau. Over half of these related to ads that included sex and nudity, discrimination or vilification. As a business owner it's your responsibility to know what you can and can't say in your ads. The *Trade Practices Act 1974* outlines the rights of advertisers and consumers to accurate, truthful and honest advertising and selling practices, and fair competition. Ads can't be misleading or give false information about a product's price or quality, among other things. For a full rundown on the rules governing advertising and selling in print, broadcast and online media, go to the Australian Competition and Consumer Commission's site <www.accc.gov.au>.

What to look for in an ad agency

There could come a time when your advertising gets too big for you to manage on your own. It's sometimes worth enlisting the help of an ad agency to get expert advice. You can look in your local phone book or online, or ask around for word-of-mouth referrals. When you're searching, look for the following things from an agency:

- *Professionalism.* Does it have the same sort of business ethos as you do? Does it stick to deadlines and deliver quality work?

- *Size.* Do you want the personal attention of a small agency or all the bells, whistles and benefits offered by a large one?

- *Experience.* Does it have an understanding of your industry and how to connect to your target market?

- *Budget.* Does the agency usually deal in six-figure ad campaigns, or smaller accounts? Make sure it can handle your budget (whether it's small or large).

- *Tracking.* How does it measure its success? Ask to see some examples of its successfully tracked campaigns.

Source: Start Local, Australia's local search engine and business directory <www.startlocal.com.au>.

See it to believe it

You can have the most honest and informative ad in the universe, but if no-one sees it, what's the point? So before you book your ad space in print or broadcast media, do your research on what will give you the biggest bang for your buck. You might think it's enough just to have a 20-second ad appear in prime time within your favourite show. But if it doesn't grab your target's attention and deliver your message quickly, you can be wasting your time and money. So know what type of carrot to dangle, and use relevant and precise words and images in every ad.

Ramp it up

Marketing experts refer to the number of times an ad appears as its 'frequency'. 'The more exposure your advertisement has to your ideal customer, the better your chances of them noticing it', states Sensis. Does your audience stop still long enough to notice ads? What sort of things do they notice? Where do they notice them? To find out these things, ask your customers before you advertise. It really will help you work out what you say, how often you need to say it and what sort of media will deliver the results you want. Maybe it's a combination of options, such as online and print. If you don't find out how your ideal customer uses media, how can you hope to get your message noticed in the crowd of ad land?

Be patient

It's really rare that an ad will result in an avalanche of sales straight away. A survey by a Canadian marketing company found that 19 per cent of the enquirers made purchases within six months (whether from the advertiser or a competitor) and 29 per cent purchased within a year. By 16 months, 43 per cent, and by 25 months, 57 per cent had made purchases. So be patient. And be consistent. Giving an ad campaign some time means you'll give your customers more of a chance to see it. And you'll have more to go on when you assess the results: how many ideal customers have called from which ads, and what they've said when they've called. Getting this sort of feedback from your customers, and actually tracking what happens, will help you plan your next move.

Online ad world

Advertising online has become a viable option for many small businesses. It's easy to set up (you can do it yourself), you can customise your ads for particular target markets and you can easily measure the results on a daily basis. Basically, it works like this:

□ You create an ad that sits within the various search engine directories (for example, Google has its own paid advertising product called Google Adwords).

□ When someone does an online search for a particular keyword or phrase that matches the ones you have nominated, your ad pops up next to the search results.

□ You only pay Google Adwords, for example, when someone clicks on your advertisement, which is linked to your website (if you don't have a site yet, Google can help you create one for the purpose of your ad).

□ To start your online ad strategy, follow these steps:

1 Have a look at a search engine company's website to see what it offers.

2 Set your budget. How much do you want to pay each time someone clicks on your ad? (On Google Adwords you can set your own maximum cost, for example, 10 cents per click.)

3 Create your online ad using the supplied templates, paying close attention to the keywords you use (this is what determines if your ad comes up next to particular search results).

> 4 Measure the results: track who's clicking on your ads and what they look for (information or to make a purchase). Make the most of the fact that you can change your ads and budget limits daily if you want to, until you get the hits you're after (that is, ones that translate into sales).

32

Question: *Where can I go when the sales go slow?*

Answer: *It's time to get back to basics.*

Snaring the sale is why you're in small business. So when sales of your product or service slow down, it can be a worry. Still, it's nothing you can't conquer, as long as you've given yourself enough time to sort out why they've slowed, and then fix the problem. Are you doing something different that's affecting your sales? Have your competitors lifted their game? Or has the market changed and you haven't changed with it? By taking the time to analyse your sales cycle, and iron out any kinks, you're giving your business the best chance to get on top of a slowing market.

The sales cycle

Generating awareness is where it all begins (and why your sales and marketing strategies should be closely aligned). The awareness turns into leads or prospects. Follow-up calls are made and customers are approached on the leads. Then any interest is converted into a sale. 'At each stage, we can get some shrinkage or leakage so that the final sales collected are only a fraction of the leads generated', says Dr Graham Godbee of the Macquarie Graduate School of Management and author of *Manage for All Seasons*. 'Marketing effectiveness and efficiency are about ensuring the leakages are minimised.' He says that in the good times, it's easy to forget about the awareness-building bit. 'Worse, sometimes we let our reputation slip and brand diminish as we just get the sales out the door.' Then, when there's a slowdown in the market or the economy as a whole, the leads shrink and the conversions get tougher and tougher.

Kathryn Conder, partner of executive and business mentoring firm Carnegie Management Group, agrees that in times of economic downturn, people's fear of buying shuts down their purchasing power. However, they'll still buy from suppliers they trust and have good communications with. 'That's why your customer communications have to be consistent and effective and have value, all the time', she says. If customers feel like they can trust you, they'll value your brand and continue to buy from you. If they feel like they're being talked into a sale, you won't keep them. 'I'm yet to see an industry where this doesn't work', adds Conder. 'People only make the decision to buy one product over another on price on a few occasions, but mostly there's something else driving the buying decision. You have to identify and overcome their objections.'

Start on the inside

A good place to start is with some training for your team. In slower sales times, Graham Godbee says it's vital 'that you and your sales staff are better than ever at converting leads to sales'. Tap into what your customers are really thinking. Godbee refers to this as your 'market intelligence data'. Train your sales team on how to measure it and report any changes back to you and the rest of your business. He also suggests you track the conversion ratio (the percentage of leads converted to sales) and conversion time (the time between the call and the sale). Train your staff so that they know how to utilise a few reporting strategies (you may already have sales reporting features on your MYOB or QuickBooks software, or you'll find a few different report templates at <www.office.microsoft.com>). Once you get them used to using the technology, they'll be able to give you the answers you need to really drive your sales.

Keep it simple

In slow sales times, it pays to focus on your current customers, suggests Kathryn Conder. 'For example, if you have a pizza business, how often do your customers come in? Is it four times a year? How could you get them to buy more?' Use your database and contact customers to ask them. And then give them a reason to come back and buy. Loyalty programs and VIP discounts often work well. And don't be afraid to ask them to make referrals to their friends, and reward them in some way when they do. You can also look at creating alliances with businesses that aren't competitors but sell to a similar target market to you. Share your market knowledge and work together to ramp up your sales. 'With the internet and emails, it's so easy and cost effective to communicate regularly with your customers', adds Conder. Do this to put structure into your sales.

Stay in control

While you're expending all this energy on reinvigorating your sales, remember to keep an eye on the whole ball game. If you grow sales quickly, and your business doesn't have the additional cash to fund an increase in assets to support the boom, you could be in trouble. It's called overtrading, says Graham Godbee. 'It often surprises business owners that growing sales could be a problem. Eventually, this is fine as you have the higher level of assets to support the increased sales. But in the short term, the extra profit from the increased sales is likely to be less than the amount that must be invested in the additional assets.' Suddenly you don't have the cash, and you need to look at funding options.

Godbee cites an example in his book *Manage for All Seasons*: 'If you are selling $2 million of goods per annum and you have a net working capital requirement of 10 per cent and the next year you grow the sales to $3 million, then you will need to fund 10 per cent of the increased sales as net working capital.

This would be 10 per cent of $1 million = $100 000. You are unlikely to make $100 000 net profit after tax from the increased sales. So although you make more profit, you are worse off on your cash flow. You run the risk of going broke by increasing sales and making more profit!' (For more on the complexities of cash flow, see question 10.) Instead, grow sales without causing you too much pain by using what Godbee refers to as the sustainable growth rate. 'It is a short-hand approximation to cash flow availability as a company changes its sales levels,' he says. (See how to work it out for your business in the breakout box below.) It can help you discipline your approach to sales growth so that no matter what sort of sales fluctuations you experience, your business will be able to handle it.

Action item: calculating your sustainable growth rate

In his book *Manage for All Seasons*, Graham Godbee tells the story of how clothing company Just Jeans used the sales growth rate to turn its business around.

'Just Jeans was a publicly listed company that was bought out by a private equity firm, Catalyst. The Catalyst business plan for Just Jeans was not pursuing large growth. Forecast growth was modest at about 5 per cent to 7 per cent per annum. Catalyst was not planning to take out any dividends. In the first year of the loan, assets were $170 million. Sales were $390 million. Equity was $50 million. Profit after tax was $7 million. No dividends were paid so all the profits were retained. These are all the inputs we require for our sustainable growth rate calculation:

Asset turnover is sales ÷ assets = 2.3 times

Sales margin is profit ÷ sales = 1.8%

So ROA (Return on Assets) = 2.3 × 1.8% = 4.14% (or profit ÷ assets = 4.1%)

Equity ÷ assets = 0.294 (highly geared)

(1−D) = 1.0 (no dividends are paid so all profits are retained)

The Sales Growth formula is (Return On Assets × (1−D)) ÷ (Equity ÷ Assets − (ROA) × (1−D)).

So for Just Jeans, Sales Growth = (0.0414 × 1.0) ÷ (0.294 − 0.0414 × 1.0) = 16.4%

So, in the first year of the loan, the company can sustain a sales growth rate of about 16 per cent. Just Jeans was trying to grow at only 5 per cent to 7 per cent, which is well under the sustainable growth rate.'

Source: *Manage for All Seasons*, by Graham Godbee.

33 Question: *How beneficial is networking?*

Answer: *It's great for business, when it's done with your end goal in mind.*

One of the challenges of being in small business is having the time to network, or get together with a group of like-minded people. Sure, you've heard about networking events, complete with cocktails and canapés, a room full of business minds and new contacts. And you can see the benefits. There's even a new idea called 'speed networking events' where people go to an event to meet as many contacts as they can in the shortest time. However, expending this sort of energy after hours is really way down on your list of priorities. But maybe it shouldn't be!

Types of networking events

Organisational psychologist Bruce Katcher says there are three types of networking events, all with different benefits:

→ groups that enable you to keep abreast of the latest developments in your field

→ career networking groups that enable you to learn more about self-marketing, interviewing and making a successful transition

→ groups that allow you to interact with prospective employers and clients.

Formal and informal opportunities offer real business benefits, if you network with purpose, says Kathryn Conder, partner of executive and business mentoring firm Carnegie Management Group. 'It's a real investment of your time, and you should think of it as you would a sales call', she adds. Do some homework before any event. Find out from the organisers who else will be there. How are they relevant to your business? What would you hope to get out of meeting them? If you have specific questions for someone you know will be there, ask the organisers to introduce you to that person.

Find your nearest network

There are a lot of networking groups online that you can be part of from the comfort of your home or office (for more on these, see question 30). For face-to-face physical contact, formal networking events are held around Australia every week. Some are put on by industry or group associations that you have to pay to join (for example, the Australian Businesswomen's Network <www.abn.org.au>, which costs $95 to join and a $20 monthly membership), while others are free. To find out what's happening in your state, check out these sites:

▫ The NSW Business Chamber <www.nswbusiness chamber.com.au> offers a Networking@Night program. Go to the site and enter the keyword 'networking' for details. All events are free for members of the Chamber; non-members need to pay for some events.

- Business Enterprise Centre Network Victoria <www.becnvic.com> has 22 Business Enterprise Centres located throughout Victoria, offering regular networking meetings (there's often a small fee involved). These BECs are part of the national Business Enterprise Centre <www.beca.org.au> network of over 130 centres.

- South Australia's Department of Trade and Economic Development (DTED) <www.business.sa.gov.au/ Events> offers a huge range of workshops and seminars. Many of them are free.

- NSW Department of State and Regional Development <http://events.smallbiz.nsw.gov.au> regularly holds a range of events, from marketing small business to safe manual handling workshops.

- Sunshine Coast Regional Council <www.business. sunshinecoast.qld.gov.au> holds a host of dedicated small business workshops which are often discounted due to government subsidies.

- The Small Business Development Corporation in Perth hosts workshops which act as information sessions and networking opportunities. Go to the 'Workshops' icon at <www.sbdc.com.au>.

- The Queensland Government offers dedicated small business training courses <www.smallbusiness solutions.qld.gov.au> (click on 'training events' under 'Services', then click on 'Start Small Business').

Find your nearest network *(cont'd)*

▫ They're a good way to learn something and network at the same time.

▫ There are private networking groups in all states. For example, in Brisbane there's a group called Networking Brisbane <www.networkingbrisbane.com>, which is worth a look, although you need to be a paid member to attend weekly breakfast meetings.

▫ Business Enterprise Centre Darwin Region offers free business workshops. Check out the calendar at <www.becnt.com.au>.

Time is money

Austrade, which hosts a lot of networking events every year (find more at <www.austrade.gov.au>; click on 'Networking opportunities' under 'About Exporting'), advises you to think about your time and money as resources. Don't waste them. For example, breakfast and early evening functions are more economical on these resources: they don't interrupt the rest of your work day as much as lunchtime events. If the networking event is a formal presentation or industry-specific seminar, Austrade recommends approaching the presenter and asking if they are able to give you a copy of the information they presented: 'take a memory stick to make it easier for the presenter to download the presentation for you'. Also ask if you can be placed on the presenter's mailing list. Collect the business cards of everyone you would like to contact in the future. Write the date and the event on the back of the card, as well as anything that you found you had in common. Writing down these details helps you remember things about the person when you go back to the cards in a week's time.

Kathryn Conder suggests allocating the time to put all this information into your database. Then analyse the event to see if it's worthwhile going again. Think about who you met. Were there any leads? Who would you like to stay in touch with? She also suggests preparing three or four fairly generic emails even before you go so that after the event you can quickly contact some of the people you've met. It might be as simple as sending them an email saying that you were reading an article you thought they may be interested in, and send them the article. 'One of my clients even sends faxes to people they've met, because no-one else sends faxes these days, so they stand out', she says.

Communication is the key

There's no point going to a networking event and standing in the corner by yourself or only talking to people you already know. The purpose of networking is to talk to people and pick up general or more specific market intelligence that could benefit your business. That's why Conder advises going to an event with a plan of who you're going to talk to, and a system to make this happen. One of your tools should be your 'elevator pitch': the three-minute rundown of who you are and what you do. Have it worked out before you go. Also work out the questions you'll ask to get people to talk about themselves. 'Business is about people and it's important to understand what's happening with them', says Kathryn Conder.

What you don't want to do, however, is become so engrossed in talking to someone that he or she is the only person you speak to during the whole event. You could miss a valuable opportunity to meet others in the room. Managing this can be a skill. Conder says that when you're talking to someone at an event, 'say to them that you're really interested in what you're discussing, so let's make time to discuss it further in the next couple of weeks'. Get their contact details and make sure you follow them up when you say you will.

Bruce Katcher says there's an art to networking, and cringes at what he calls the 'naive networker' approach. These people 'spend the meeting darting from conversation to conversation passing out their business cards to everyone and saying things like, "let me know if you hear of anybody who needs my services", and "call me if you hear of anything for me"'. He thinks that this is a waste of time as 'they have not yet earned the respect of people to warrant referrals'.

A better idea, he says, is to go to networking meetings with the mindset of, 'how can I help others at the meeting'. 'There are many ways you can help others', says Katcher. 'You can provide introductions; recommend books or websites; provide information about people, companies, or trends; or simply listen and offer emotional support.' Networking is about developing relationships and opening yourself, and your business, up to opportunities. Call it your right-time, right-place strategy: now that someone has met you, he or she might get in touch in a few months, or years, when in need of your services. Look at networking as an investment in your future business and you'll get the most out of every event.

Part V

Nutting out the legals and logistics

This section is all about helping you negotiate your way through the minefield of general compliance, legal and logistics issues that affect small business. Owning a small business involves a stack of responsibility: to your customers, your team and yourself. The trick is to know how much you need to do, and how to stay sane through the process.

Depending on your industry sector and your product or service, you might have compliance and occupational health and safety issues that you need to be aware of and protect yourself against. Plus, once you employ someone, you have workers' compensation and superannuation obligations to contend with. The information here will help but, again, you should always get professional advice from your lawyer or solicitor.

34 **Question:** *Should I buy or rent my premises?*

Answer: *There are pluses and minuses for both options when it comes to commercial property.*

Some of Australia's most profitable small businesses say they owe part of their success to their real estate portfolio. They buy their office, retail shop or industrial site (the three main types of commercial property), and then use the property as equity with the bank when they want to grow their business. Often, they end up owning more than one commercial property. But is this sort of strategy right for everyone? Renting also can make commercial sense in certain business circumstances. So which option is really better for your business?

A deductible decision

Often the decision to rent or buy your business premises comes down to a financial one. For a start, there's what you can claim at tax time. According to regional director of H&R Block Frank Brass, you'll get tax advantages for both buying a commercial property and for renting. He says that as an owner you can claim some of the ownership costs and interest, and write off building costs, if appropriate. 'As a renter you claim the rent and outgoings (insurance, rates and so on). The fixtures and fittings are claimed by either buyers or renters, whoever pays for the work', he adds. There are certainly pluses and minuses for both options, and you should consider them all before you decide one way or the other.

The buying pluses

Owning your commercial property means that you have free rein to do what you want to do with a building or land (if you need to expand or develop your business). Just make sure you've investigated the local council planning laws and building permit requirements to find out what's allowed and what's not before you buy. Another plus is that by buying, you're adding to the assets of your company, and you can benefit from the increased value of the property. If you later decide to move on to another property but still keep the first one, you'll be able to get the benefits of renting it out, assuming you've bought in a good location.

Offices offer the lowest yield of the three main types of commercial property, according to Peter Koulizos, a property researcher and lecturer at the University of South Australia. 'Over the past 30 years, offices have averaged a 7 per cent return but currently are returning 6 per cent', he says. 'Since 1980, retail property has returned an average of 9 per cent but currently is returning just above 6 per cent. Industrial property is the most volatile with regards to returns. Yields are currently around 7 per cent.' The message is simple: understand the returns on different types of commercial property before you buy. Then, if you do end up renting it out down the track, you'll know what you can expect to earn.

The buying minuses

You have to come up with the deposit for the property, and the bank might want you to use your home as security. Make sure you're prepared for this. Annual bills, such as council rates and all maintenance and upkeep costs, become your problem when you own your premises. Before you buy, have a good look at the state of the building to make sure it's structurally sound (you don't need surprises). Also, take interest rates into your purchasing consideration: what might be a good mortgage now might not be so good when interest rates rise. Do your budget and be prepared. Frank Brass adds that you should think forward to the day you may want to sell up and move premises (for example, if you want to expand further, or if the location isn't attracting the clients or customers it once was). If you don't think it will be easy to resell down the track, maybe you should consider another location to buy as the last thing you want is to be stuck with a property that's not suitable for you, or anyone else.

The renting pluses

Leasing isn't as expensive up front as buying (there's only a rental bond and rent to pay, not a deposit and a mortgage). You mostly share the expenses of maintenance with the landlord (they will often fix anything major that goes wrong with the property). You can know exactly what you're up for every year in terms of rent, electricity and other property incidentals. However, Peter Koulizos suggests you read the lease carefully and understand the terms and conditions, the GST implications and who is responsible for the outgoings (expenses) of the building. Always pass things by your solicitor. Another plus of renting is that when your lease is up for renewal, you can try to negotiate a better deal. One of the other big benefits is that you can move if there are any dramas with your landlord or the property. Go into every lease knowing how much notice you have to give if you decide to move on.

The renting minuses

Both renting and buying lock you into the property for a period of time, but a lease is less flexible as you are locked in for the lease period, cautions Brass. Plus you're not building the asset for your business. You could also be at the mercy of your landlord as to how much your rent goes up each year. If the owner wants to sell, you run the risk of being turfed out by a new owner. And you don't have the flexibility to do what you want with the building, office or retail space. If you're leasing in a shopping complex that relies on what Koulizos calls an 'anchor tenant' (such as a supermarket that draws people to the complex), and this tenant decides to move, your business might be significantly affected.

Action item: who can you call?

It's a really good idea to get some advice from your accountant or business adviser: they'll help you work out whether your specific business should buy or rent its premises. Once you have some figures in front of you, call three local real estate agents (search for them in the *Yellow Pages* or online) to find out the types of commercial property they have on their books, and the going rate for renting and buying. This will help you crunch some more numbers on what's going to work best for your business.

Questions to ask

Before you jump in to the commercial real estate market to rent or buy, think about your type of business, the size of the property you need, and your plans for growth. Are you looking to stay in this premises for a long time, or will you hold onto it for only a few years before you're ready to move on? Does the building you're looking to buy comply with health and safety standards? Will buying the property be a good investment, regardless of whether your business is in it or not? These are just a few of the many things to factor in to your decision. Spend the time going through the preceding list of pros and cons, and then develop your own list. Take it to your accountant and get his or her advice. And remember, what's good for the business around the corner mightn't be right for you.

Buying or leasing cars and equipment

Every business is different, and the decision whether to buy or lease motor vehicles and office equipment such as photocopiers, faxes, computers and furniture is up to you. The Victorian Department of Innovation, Industry and Regional Development (DIIRD) has this list of leasing pros and cons to consider on its Business Victoria website.

Advantages of leasing:

- costs are more spread out and can become part of your cash flow

- as a condition of your lease, rates can be fixed for the period of the lease

- for the lessee, lease payments can be claimed as tax deductions

- maintenance costs are usually the responsibility of the owner.

Disadvantages of leasing:

- over the life of an item, leasing can end up costing you more than buying

- buying is a single payment, but leasing is an ongoing cost you need to allow for

- the lessee cannot claim depreciation of equipment as a tax deduction

- there may be penalties for breaking the lease agreement; for example, missing a payment.

Attributed to Business Victoria <www.businessvictoria.vic.gov.au>.

35 Question: *Where do I start with OH&S issues?*
Answer: *Start by talking to your team.*

Occupational health and safety (OH&S) is all about you and your employees being safe at work. The flipside is a business owner's nightmare: one of your employees gets hurt and suddenly you're potentially in a lot of trouble. Not only do you lose productivity while he or she is home recuperating, but if you don't have rock solid OH&S procedures in place, you and your business could be staring down the barrel of a lawsuit (see more on this in question 41). Even if you're the only one in your business, you need to be aware of OH&S. For example, the Australian Government says at <www.business.gov.au> that 'you must ensure that your business doesn't create health and safety problems for your customers and the general public'.

It's one part of your business to take extremely seriously. Every year in Australia, according to Safe Work Australia's *Compendium of Workers Compensation Statistics* <www.safeworkaustralia.com.au>, it's estimated that more people die from workplace accidents and injuries than on our roads. Then there are the thousands of people who have time off work because of sickness or injury incurred in their jobs (see more workers' compensation statistics in question 37). This is why each state and territory government has developed specific OH&S legislation that every business owner is legally bound to adhere to. Under OH&S regulations and codes of conduct (which vary slightly from state to state), you have to try to keep you and your team safe and healthy at work.

What is being safe?

There's a checklist on <www.business.gov.au> which states that 'under OH&S legislation you are obliged to provide safe premises, safe machinery and materials, safe systems of work, information, instruction, training and supervision, and a suitable working environment and facilities'. Dr Maree Bernoth, an OH&S researcher and lecturer at Charles Sturt University, suggests that safety should also mean having a regard for your employees' and your welfare. 'It's about having a genuine interest in working together to ensure people go home from work feeling enhanced, empowered and secure after a day on the job, both physically and psychologically', she says.

If it's this easy, why do so many small business owners worry about addressing the issue of OH&S? Bernoth thinks the first reason is ignorance of where to go to find out information, what to do and how to comply. 'Then there's the fear of not complying, with small business owners concerned that they might get it wrong', she says. It is a complex area, and there's a perception that complying is expensive (in actual fact, you can do a lot of it for free: see following). Also, many owners think that they have to do it all themselves. 'But they're missing the point that OH&S has to be about inclusion: you need to systematically go through a consultation process with your employees because they're the ones who will implement the policies', adds Bernoth. 'It's essential to get their input; otherwise they will not take ownership of any OH&S procedures.'

How do I start?

Go to the website of your state or territory OH&S authority (see the breakout box, p. 165, for contact details). Each authority has step-by-step checklists and information that walks you through the compliance process (covering things such as emergency procedures, chemical safety, machinery and equipment safety and manual handling policies). All the information you need is there and also on the Safe Work Australia website <www.safeworkaustralia.gov.au>. It shouldn't take more than a couple of hours to go through it all. There are also safety action plan templates for you to use so that when you get to writing your business's own OH&S policy, you'll be meeting your legal requirements. You can also get a free advisory visit from someone from your OH&S

authority to point you in the right direction. Plus, your local Business Enterprise Centre <www.beca.org.au> offers free advice on OH&S compliance issues.

Every OH&S investigation should start with your staff. 'You shouldn't ignore or exclude them from the decision-making, or the process of writing your OH&S policy and procedures', says Bernoth. 'If the people are expected to carry out tasks in a certain way, they should be given a say in the procedures.' Talk to your staff about the issues and hazards they can see at work. What sort of training do they need to get them over the legal OH&S line? It might be in chemicals, manual handling or confined space education. Once you identify what's needed, you can organise training through your state WorkCover organisation or Business Enterprise Centre.

What if I don't comply?

Basically, not having compliant OH&S procedures means you can be prosecuted and fined by your state or territory authority. So make the time. You need compliant OH&S policies in place so that you're covered legally, and entitled to apply for workers' compensation (see question 41) if something does happen at work to one of your employees. With all the online tools at your state OH&S authority, combined with your intimate knowledge of your business, it shouldn't take you long to create what Bernoth calls 'a systematic approach to OH&S'. By assessing what's needed, writing it down in an action plan (some of the things might be short term or long term) and then regularly evaluating it to see how you're going, you will be continuously improving your OH&S performance. And if you're really stretched and can't find the time to find out the information you need, get a trusted employee to start the process for you. This person can get the buy-in of the rest of the team to determine what they all do, what they all need and identify any issues. 'The most solid OH&S situation comes when the employer and employees work together', adds Bernoth.

WorkCover contacts

Each state and territory OH&S authority has its own website and contact phone numbers. It's worth giving it a call to find out what you need to do for your business to adhere to OH&S legislation. Here are the main websites and numbers you will need (there are others relating particularly to the mining sector). Write down your relevant authority's contact details and put this where everyone who works in your business can see it.

◻ Australian Capital Territory: Office of Regulatory Services (ORS) WorkCover <www.workcover.act. gov.au>; phone (02) 6205 0200 or (02) 6207 3000.

◻ New South Wales: WorkCover New South Wales <www.workcover.nsw.gov.au>; phone 13 10 50.

◻ Northern Territory: NT WorkSafe <www.worksafe.nt. gov.au>; phone 1800 019 115.

◻ Queensland: Department of Justice & Attorney General <www.deir.qld.gov.au/workplace/index.htm>; phone 1300 369 915 or (07) 3225 2000.

◻ South Australia: SafeWork SA <www.safework. sa.gov.au>; phone 1300 365 255.

◻ Tasmania: WorkCover Tasmania <www.workcover. tas.gov.au>; phone 1300 366 322 (inside Tasmania).

◻ Victoria: WorkSafe Victoria <www.workcover.vic. gov.au>; phone 1800 136 089 or (03) 9641 1444.

◻ Western Australia: WorkSafe WA <www.worksafe. wa.gov.au>; phone 1300 307 877.

Source: Safe Work Australia <www.safeworkaustralia.gov.au>.

36 Question: *So many insurances seem like a waste of money. Are they?*

Answer: *It really is a case of you can't afford not to be insured.*

The insurance industry is awash with horror stories to get you motivated to take out insurance: check out the 'Understanding the risks' section of the Investment and Financial Services Association's (IFSA) site Lifewise <www.lifewise.org.au> for some fairly hairy health stats. However, the reality is that things *can* go wrong, both personally and professionally. It's up to you, as the business owner, to work out what types of insurances you really can and can't do without. And that's the hard part. There are literally hundreds of products on offer and they all vary in price, depending on what it is you're insuring.

Once you sign up and those monthly instalments are added to your list of outgoings, it can feel like you're throwing money into something you don't think you'll ever see the benefit of. The sky's not falling on your business, and you don't foresee it will be any time soon. According to the Lifewise site, it's this 'she'll be right' attitude that has resulted in only 31 per cent of Australians having income protection insurance (from a survey by market researchers TNS and the IFSA), while 83 per cent insure their car (from AAMI data). It's also a hard thing to get your head around if you've just started a small business, and you have no idea how much your income will be, let alone how much everything else will be worth. But imagine if something serious did happen to your health. How would this impact your business, your income and your family? Have you mitigated your risks?

According to the Australian Government's business portal <www.business.gov.au>, there are three areas of insurance: assets and revenue insurance; people insurance; and liability insurance. The type of industry sector you're in will determine your specific business insurance requirements. If you're unsure what you need, get some advice from your financial planner or accountant on insurance types and the minimum amounts you should be insured for (so that you're adequately covered but don't waste money). Also, some industry associations have bulk insurance deals that you can tap in to. Call your specific association or industry rep for more details.

Insurance brokers

If you don't know where to start when it comes to insurance for your business, it can be useful to speak to an insurance broker. Make sure they have business insurance experience. Usually, they're familiar with a range of products, as well as the companies that can package up insurance plans to make the whole thing simpler for your business. The National Insurance Brokers Association has a list of accredited brokers nationally on its website <www. niba.com.au> under the 'Need a Broker' link. Here's what Business Victoria suggests you ask each broker before you make your choice:

- What are their qualifications?

- Who will service your account?

- How many insurance companies do they have access to?

- What experience do they have with your size and type of business?

- What are their services?

- How do they charge?

- Can they supply you with referees—especially those with your type of business?

Insurance brokers *(cont'd)*

◻ Are they members of the National Insurance Brokers Association and do they subscribe to the General Insurance Brokers' Code?

Attributed to Business Victoria <www.businessvictoria.vic.gov.au>.

Asset and revenue insurance

It's definitely worth protecting your major assets, particularly ones that are vital to your business operations. There's your building, its contents and your stock, which can be insured 'against fire and other perils such as earthquake, lightning, storms, impact, malicious damage and explosion', according to <www.business.gov.au>. You can insure your business against burglary (really relevant for retailers), business interruption or loss of profits, and machinery breakdown. Then there's fidelity guarantee, which the Australian Government site says 'covers losses resulting from misappropriation by employees who embezzle or steal'. On top of all this, there are four different types of motor vehicle insurance to consider: compulsory third party (injury), third party property damage, third party fire and theft, and comprehensive insurance, which you might be asked to sign up for if you're buying or leasing a car through a finance company.

People insurance

Again, there are many options to consider when it comes to your employees. But let's start with insurance for a vital person in your business: you. First, there's your life insurance. According to the Australian Securities & Investments Commission (ASIC), you can choose from investment-style funds 'where you contribute over a certain time and get back your investment plus interest earnings at the maturity date'. Other fund styles will cover the risk of things going wrong.

To work out how much you should be insuring your life for, ASIC suggests that you sit down and consider your financial commitments and how long you think they'll last (include your children's education in the mix). A professional financial adviser can help, or go to ASIC's consumer website called Fido (go to <www.fido.asic.gov.au> and then click on the 'About financial products' section).

ASIC also recommends that you consider income protection insurance for the simple fact that your business often needs you to be able to work. The National Insurance Brokers Association <www.niba.com.au> agrees. 'Some income protection policies are particularly appropriate to small business as they can provide, in addition to income replacement for the business operator, cover for overheads incurred by the business during the proprietor's incapacity.' This might help you to hire someone to work in the business while you're recovering. States NIBA: 'An example of this would be a doctor who brings in a locum to keep the practice operating'.

When it comes to your staff, you also have to look at workers' compensation and superannuation. Workers' compensation is covered by separate state and territory legislation, with varying guidelines. ASIC suggests you contact your state workers' comp organisation for details of what's relevant to your business (see the 'WorkCover contacts' box in question 35).

If you're self-employed, you're not covered by workers' compensation. Instead, you can insure yourself for personal accident and illness. In terms of superannuation, there are certain rules you are obliged to adhere to for all of your employees. Plus there's your own super to think about for the day you do retire. (There's so much superannuation information to consider, it's warranted its own section: see question 38 for details.)

Action item: insurance needs

There's an Insurance Needs calculator at the Lifewise site <www.lifewise.org.au/calculator/main.html>. Developed by Rice Warner Actuaries, of Sydney, it helps you quickly work out an estimate of your insurance requirements. While it is specifically aimed at life and income protection insurance, it's a good way to launch you into the world of insurance.

Liability insurance

Your type of business will determine the sort of liability insurance you'll need. At <www.business.gov.au>, the Australian Government outlines three liability insurances: public liability, professional indemnity and product liability. Public liability insurance 'protects you and your business against the financial risk of being found liable to a third party for death or injury, loss or damage of property or "pure economic" loss resulting from your negligence'.

Professional indemnity insurance protects you from being sued if something happens after you've given someone advice. You'll also be covered if a client or customer 'suffers a loss — either material, financial or physical — directly attributed to negligent acts'. Product liability insurance is relevant for small businesses where the goods are fragile. If one of your products injures another person or business, you'll also be covered. For more information on all these insurances, you can access a web directory of government agencies and business associations through the <www.business.gov.au> website (click on the 'Insurance' link in the 'Essential business information' section of the site).

The last word

If you actually signed up for every bit of insurance on offer, you'd go broke. So sit down and assess what the biggest risks are to your business. If you don't know what they are, how can you hope to insure against them? Prioritising the areas that should be covered by insurance can also help you budget for what needs to be paid first, and what could possibly wait.

37 **Question:** *Will a workers' compensation claim affect my business?*

Answer: *Keeping up with your workers' comp responsibilities will protect you financially.*

Just sometimes, regardless of the sound occupational health and safety processes and procedures you've put in place, accidents happen. As a result, one of your staff could be hurt at work. That's when you really need to be up to date with your workers' compensation responsibilities. Your aim as an employer is to create a safe and healthy working environment, and how you deal with accidents reflects on your business culture. Keeping up with your workers' comp commitments, and any new legislation that comes up, also works in your business's financial favour too: you're protecting yourself from being liable for any compensation claims, both now and in the future.

What is workers' compensation?

Basically, workers' compensation is another part of the OH&S laws that require injured workers to have access to first aid, monetary compensation while they're recuperating and a return-to-work rehabilitation program. (If you're in the OH&S wilderness, and don't yet have suitable strategies for your business, turn back to question 35.) Workers' compensation comes in to play when someone suffers from a work-related injury or disease.

Take the case of JT. He recently tripped on a loose tile while doing the security rounds in a large office block. He strained his back, and was laid up in bed for a month. While he was recuperating, he still got his usual wage, paid by his workers' comp fund, which also covered all his doctor's bills. All up, his injury would have cost him thousands of dollars, but neither JT nor his employer were out of pocket a cent. And he was one of the lucky ones (he recovered quickly from his injury). Safe Work Australia's *Compendium of Workers' Compensation Statistics* estimates that there were 132 055 serious workers' compensation claims in 2006–07: that's 14 claims per 1000 employees. Many of them received lump sum payments through workers' comp for permanent disabilities and impairment. It's serious stuff.

Who has it?

Individuals don't pay for their own workers' compensation insurance. It's up to you as their employer to do it on their behalf. According to a comprehensive report published by Safe Work Australia entitled *Comparison of Workers' Compensation Arrangements in Australia and New Zealand* (you'll find it under 'Workers' Compensation' at <www.safeworkaustralia. gov.au>), as of June 2007, 89.2 per cent of all Australian employees were covered by workers' compensation. They could be full time, part time, casuals or piece workers. Your workers' compensation premium doesn't cover contractors and subcontractors, notes Dr Maree Bernoth, OH&S researcher and lecturer at Charles Sturt University. If you use a subcontractor or contractor, she says you should sight their workers' comp policy and check it's valid for the period of the work. If it's not, you could be sued if an accident happens. 'You'll also need to demonstrate to them that your premises are safe for them to come into. This could be as simple as giving them an orientation to the building or work site', she adds.

You, as the business owner, are not eligible for workers' compensation, except if you have set up a company and you're a director of the company. As such, you are classed as an employee and you can claim against the company's workers' comp insurance. 'However, if you make a claim, your future premiums for workers' comp insurance are affected', says Bernoth. If your business has been set up as a sole trader or partnership, you should look into personal accident and illness insurance, or income protection, just in case you're injured at work.

Your first aid plan

An essential part of being a safe and healthy workplace is to have an adequate first aid plan, just in case something does happen (most state and territory OH&S authorities have these plans available online; see question 35 for contact details). Australian Red Cross <www.redcross.org.au> suggests that every business should start their plan by buying a first aid kit (prices start at about $40 for a basic kit, up to over $200, and you can buy them online; click on 'First Aid courses and products', then 'First aid kits'). The kit size and contents will depend on the number of employees and the statutory OH&S requirements for your business, which takes in your level of risk determined by a risk assessment (for example, a small retail store with one or two people only needs a Workplace C Kit, while a construction site with over 25 employees needs an A+ Kit). If you employ more than 10 people, you will need at least one first aider (with a current Senior First Aid Certificate) available to staff. Businesses with less than 10 people could be compliant by having an adequate first aid kit on the premises. Always check the requirements for your specific business.

What do I need to know?

As an employer, you are legally bound to pay workers' compensation insurance premiums on behalf of everyone employed in your business. It's an offence under state and territory legislation to try to get out of paying it, and compliance officers are paid to find offenders. Failure to pay workers' comp insurance for your employees could see you slapped with fines of several thousand dollars per employee (depending on the state or territory jurisdiction you're under), which can be backdated from the moment you don't pay.

How much are premiums?

The average premium varies from state to state and between industry sectors. Generally, it's anywhere between about 1 and 6 per cent of payroll. Your insurance premium is calculated by a licensed insurance company based on an estimate of the wages you'll pay out in the next year. There's a minimum wage amount which qualifies employees to be eligible to make a claim for workers' compensation if they're injured at work, which again varies (in NSW, for example, it's $7500 per year), so check with your state organisation for details. It pays to factor this all in when you're calculating your current and future wages and salaries expenses. 'Premiums can be reduced with a good record and increased for a poor one', says Bernoth. It pays to be safe.

How do I sign up?

You apply for workers' comp insurance from a licensed insurer. You can find out who they are and how to contact them by going to your state or territory's WorkCover website. Once the paperwork is all filled out, you'll be covering your staff for workers' compensation. You then have to let staff know who the workers' compensation insurer is, and put its contact details up on noticeboards so all employees can see them. If any accidents happen at work, make sure you contact the insurer, and most importantly document everything about the accident so that you can attach the details to any claim.

What happens in a claim?

It's the employee's responsibility to let you know about an injury at work and to get a workers' compensation medical certificate from a doctor. You'll have workers' comp claim forms that your insurer has given you: get your employee to fill one out. Keep all paperwork together (including your report of the accident), including the medical certificate. Then send it off to your insurer. If you haven't filled out the forms correctly, or you've missed something out, they'll quickly tell you and send it back for amendments. The insurance company will contact you to let you know what your employee is entitled to, and organise payment of the claim. The more information you have from the start of a claim, the smoother the whole process will be.

Getting back to work

Lost productivity: that's what hits your business the hardest when one of your valued employees is injured. The various state and territory WorkCover organisations know it too. They all have policies to try to help workers get back on the job as quickly as they can, even if it means they come back to light duties for a while. It's good for their recovery, and great for team morale. To learn more about the back-to-work policy of your state authority (see the breakout box on p. 165 for contact details), give it a call so that you can set the expectations with your worker and the rest of your team.

38 **Question:** *Exactly what are my superannuation obligations, and are there any shortcuts?*

Answer: *Paying the right amount of super on behalf of your staff is something you need to take seriously.*

The moment you employ someone, you have to take superannuation seriously. The Australian Government's tax laws say that every working person is entitled to super, which is a way of helping them save for their retirement. Your part in the process is to pay what's known as the superannuation guarantee for all the people you employ. Your super guarantee payments are tax deductible, but it can be a time-consuming process if you don't know your obligations, the paperwork that needs filling out, and what happens if you don't do it properly.

The best place to start your super snooping is with the Australian Taxation Office's website <www.ato.gov.au/super>. The 'Employers super essentials' section of the site won't shortcut your obligations, but it will help make the whole process easier for you. And if this means saving you time, that's a good thing. Here's a rundown of what the ATO says you need to know about your super obligations. You can call it on 13 10 20 for more information, or call your accountant, who can also give you advice on the more confusing parts.

Your super obligations

As an employer you are bound by Commonwealth legislation to make superannuation contributions for almost all employees (full time, part time, casual and some eligible contractors). According to the ATO, eligible employees 'are aged between 18 and 70 (although they can be under 18), are paid $450 (before tax) or more in a calendar month, and work full time, part time or on a casual basis for more than 30 hours in a week. You may also have to pay super for any employees who are visiting Australia on a temporary resident visa'. You start making super contributions, known as the superannuation guarantee, for an employee no later than 28 days from the day he or she starts working for you.

The current amount of compulsory super contributions is a minimum of 9 per cent of an employee's 'ordinary time earnings'. The ATO defines this as 'what they earn for their ordinary hours of work'. It's on top of an employee's salary or wage. The contributions have to be made at least four times a year by due dates that have been set by the ATO. You pay them into your employees' chosen super fund (if they are eligible to choose their own fund, which you can check on the ATO site). If an employee doesn't nominate a fund after the first 28 days of employment with you, you have to pay the superannuation guarantee into your employer-nominated fund (the Tax Office also calls this your default fund).

The paperwork

First, find out from new employees which super fund they want their super guarantee to go into (and get them to provide you with the super fund's contact details). Also get their tax file number so that you can quote it to their super fund. Then, you need to get your employees to fill out a *Standard choice form* from the ATO. You can download these forms or order them by calling the ATO's publications ordering service (phone 1300 720 092 and quote NAT number 13080). Keep a few *Standard choice forms* on hand in case an existing eligible employee also wants to change the super fund his or her guarantee is going into.

When it comes to your records, the ATO stipulates: 'You must keep records (for five years) that adequately show the amount of super that was paid for each employee. You should also keep any documents that helped you calculate the level of super you paid...and records that affect your liability, such as advice from trustees about the funds to which you are contributing'. There are penalties of up to $3300 for an individual and $16500 for a corporation if you don't keep your records accurate and up to date. 'If you are required to pay superannuation under an award (state or federal), you may have additional recordkeeping obligations and you should check your relevant award or regulations', asserts the ATO.

How to do it right

Make sure you always have copies of the forms you need for new employees. Set up the superannuation payment process for your business so that it's part of your quarterly outgoings. 'If you are not sure what award or industrial agreement, if any, an employee is covered by, phone the workplace relations department in your state or territory', suggests the ATO.

Action item: super calculator tools

There are a number of superannuation cal-culator tools you can access for free on the Australian Taxation Office website <www.ato.gov.au/business>; click on 'Find a rate or calculator' then 'Superannuation'. You remain anonymous when using these tools:

- The Superannuation Guarantee Contributions Calculator will help you work out how much your super obligations are for each employee.

- The Superannuation Guarantee Eligibility Decision tool helps you check if your employees are eligible for superannuation guarantee contributions.

- The Superannuation Guarantee Charge Statement and Calculator tool will work out your superannuation guarantee charge if you've underpaid your super obligations; the ATO estimates it will take you five to 10 minutes to complete per employee for each quarter.

If you don't do it

Under Australia's superannuation laws, you're expected to do the right thing as an employer. If you don't, the Australian Taxation Office *will* come calling. You can be penalised with a 'superannuation guarantee charge' for not paying enough of your super obligations (maybe your calculations for the 9 per cent of an employee's 'ordinary time earnings' aren't correct), or you pay after the quarterly cut-off date, or you pay the super into the wrong fund (know as a 'choice liability').

According to the ATO, the super guarantee charge is made up of three parts: 'The super guarantee shortfall amounts (including any choice liability), interest on that amount (10 per cent per annum), and an administration fee ($20 per employee per quarter)'. If you think you might be up for this charge, you should download a *Superannuation guarantee charge statement—quarterly* form from the ATO website. If you don't resolve the matter and pay this charge by the due date, 'you will then have to pay the general interest charge (the rate of this is updated quarterly)', states the ATO. The best idea is to always pay your super obligations on time and to the right place, and you'll never have to worry about paying penalties.

39 **Question:** *Is going green something that's going to benefit my business?*

Answer: *Start with some easy 'green' business practices and see how much money you save.*

Green business is the new buzz. With climate change an ever-encroaching threat, many small businesses would like to look at what they can do to be more environmentally aware. The problem for you is that you think getting on the bandwagon will cost you money. And there's no time to do it. What difference could your business make, anyway? You mightn't make a huge difference on your own, but think of your business as one important part of Australia's dynamic small business sector. Research from Edith Cowan University in Western Australia suggests that the combined carbon footprint of the small business collective is estimated to be as much as 70 per cent of global pollution. So while you mightn't be able to make a huge dent in our environmental woes on your own, if you and all your entrepreneurial friends started a few small (and cost-effective) green initiatives as part of doing business, it could certainly help.

Easy ways to make a difference

You don't have to install masses of solar panels or reconfigure your whole office to make a difference to climate change (although if you are retro-fitting your office, it's worth seeing if there are any government 'green' grants for you to do it: see question 18). GreenBizCheck <www.greenbizcheck.com> has come up with a multitude of ways you and your staff can make a difference:

→ *Recycle*. Most people only think about paper and cardboard. But have you ever thought about what else your office could recycle (depending on your local council)? Think about other things around your office such as glass bottles and jars, aluminium and steel cans, empty aerosols, milk and juice cartons, plastic cups and plastic take-away containers. Have specially marked recycling bins for each of these to make it easy for your staff.

→ *Switch things off*. According to GreenBizCheck, about 10 per cent of the total global electrical appliance energy consumption is wasted on stand-by energy. Turn everything, including printers, scanners and photocopiers, off at the power point at the end of each day. And turn computer monitors off if you're leaving your desk for more than a few minutes: the monitor uses up to two-thirds of a computer's energy.

→ *New equipment.* Buy office equipment and appliances with a high energy rating. Make sure your new photocopiers and printers work well using recycled paper (ask your supplier).

→ *Unplug chargers.* If phone, walkie-talkie, torch and drill chargers are plugged in and the switch is on, energy is being consumed.

→ *Work from home.* Let your employees work from home regularly. According to GreenBizCheck, a commute of two hours a day means that in 40 years you'll have spent 2.3 years commuting. Think of those fuel costs!

Benefits to your bottom line

You might be interested in some of these statistics from GreenBizCheck:

→ Leaving a computer screen on for just one night uses up enough energy to microwave six dinners.

→ A typical desktop PC will pump out 80 watts of heat, forcing air cons to work even harder—thus wasting even more energy.

→ A computer left on 24/7 costs approximately $95 a year to run. If this PC is switched off before going home and at weekends, this can be reduced to $20. A hundred PCs switched off when not in use will save around $7500 a year.

→ Leaving the lights on, combined with computers left on standby, can double a company's energy bill.

→ An energy-efficient bulb can use up to 80 per cent less energy and lasts about eight times longer than an ordinary incandescent bulb. Although it costs about 10 times more than an ordinary $1 bulb it will save over $80 in electricity.

→ You can save $200 a year by using rechargeable batteries instead of disposables in just one CD player used two hours a day.

→ Increasing the air-conditioner temperature at home by 1°C in the summer and reducing the temperature by 1°C in the winter will save around 10 per cent off your energy bill. Use this same strategy in your office.

Where to go for more info

At the time of writing there was no legislation to make small businesses report their energy use, waste disposal practices and carbon emissions. However, the sector is quickly moving on to the federal, state and territory governments' environment radar. Every business and industry sector is different, so get in first and learn as much as you can about policies that might impact your business practices in the future.

→ The Department of the Environment, Water, Heritage and the Arts's website <www.environment.gov.au/about/programs> lists government policy developments and it also has information on any new 'green' funding opportunities.

→ If you're in an environmentally sensitive sector, such as farming or fisheries, you might need to apply for permits under the federal government's *Environment Protection and Biodiversity Conservation Act 1999* (EPBC Act). You'll find the Act at <www.environment.gov.au/epbc>.

→ You can get an independent environmental audit by going to the 'Environmental management' part of the <www.business.gov.au> site. Or go to the GreenBizCheck website, which offers an online office assessment: <www.greenbizcheck.com/free-office-assessment/>.

→ If you want to have your product or service recognised as being environmentally friendly, go to the Department of Resources, Energy and Tourism site at <www.ret.gov.au>.

→ You can register your product or service as 'greenhouse friendly' and utilise the marketing advantage (go to <www.climatechange.gov.au> and click on 'Emissions monitoring' then 'Greenhouse Friendly').

→ Find out how much electricity you can save at work by using the GreenBizCheck energy savings calculator <www.greenbizcheck.com>.

→ The Queensland Government's Department of Employment, Industry Development and Innovation has developed an online diagnostic tool on its Smart Small Business website (go to <www.sdi.qld.gov.au> and click on the 'Online diagnostic tools' link in the 'Online services' box. Then click on the 'Climate change quiz'). The quiz takes about 10 minutes to do. You might be motivated into action after doing it.

Action item: what's your carbon footprint?

There are many online tools that now help you calculate your small business's carbon footprint. Here are three of the best:

▫ The Carbon Neutral Business Carbon Calculator is at <www.carbonneutral.com>.

▫ Edith Cowan University offers links to a greenhouse calculator and a driving carbon calculator through their Small and Medium Enterprise Research Centre (SMERC). Go to <www.business.ecu.edu.au/schools/man/smerc> then click on 'Green Advantage for Small Business' and then the 'online calculators' link.

▫ Climate Positive has a Small Business Calculator at <www.climatepositive.org/measure>.

40 **Question:** *What are fair trading laws and how do they apply to me?*

Answer: *Fair trading laws and business codes protect you and your customers.*

Owning your own business is possibly the best thing you've done. So don't let the challenges of all the legal bits to do with supplying a product or service overwhelm you. Instead, look at legal knowledge as another form of insurance. Be up with the laws that are relevant to your industry sector. Most of them have been set down by the federal, state and territory governments, and you can access all the information online (start with the web addresses included in this section). No amount of reading, however, can prepare you totally for the day that someone makes a claim against your product or service (for the legalities that relate to the people side of your business, see question 41). So always get professional legal advice from your solicitor or lawyer.

Codes of Practice

Codes of Practice are the standards of conduct that are expected of businesses in Australia. From having clean staff toilets to alerting staff to the dangers of handling hazardous substances, the industry codes cover just about every health and safety area in your workplace. Did you know that according to one NSW Code of Practice, you must have one toilet for every 20 males (and one urinal for every 25 males) and one toilet for every 15 female employees? While Codes of Practice aren't legally enforceable, they can be used as evidence against you in other matters. As they're regulated at a Commonwealth and state and territory level, you should start by going to your state's OH&S website (see question 35 for details). Also check with your specific industry association to see if there are any Codes of Conduct that apply specifically to your type of business. Two other organisations with valuable information are:

→ Safe Work Australia for a list of National Codes: <www.safeworkaustralia.gov.au> (click on 'OHS standards' under 'Health & Safety').

→ Business Enterprise Centre Australia for general information: <www.beca.org.au> or call 1300 363 551 for contact details of your nearest Business Enterprise Centre (BEC).

Fair trading

You are legally bound by federal, state and territory legislation to conduct your trade in a fair and efficient way. The Trade Practices Act (TPA) is the federal law, and it's administered by the Australian Competition and Consumer Commission (ACCC). According to <www.business.gov.au>, the Trade Practices Act 'deals with almost all aspects of the marketplace: dealings with suppliers, wholesalers, retailers, competitors and customers', covering everything from product safety and labelling to mergers and acquisitions of companies. For example, all food producers have strict guidelines for product recalls. Each state and territory government then has more specific fair trading legislation, which you need to be aware of when conducting your business. For all fair trading information, start at:

→ The ACCC's website <www.accc.gov.au>. It contains a free publication called *Small Business and the Trade Practices Act* which goes through all of your rights and obligations under the *Trade Practices Act 1974*. You can also call the ACCC's small business helpline on 1300 302 021.

→ The Australian Government's business advisory portal <www.business.gov.au>. It has links to all state and territory fair trading offices.

Action item: handling customer complaints

Working out how to deal with your customers in good times and bad is the secret to success. The Queensland Office of Fair Trading has these tips to deal effectively with customer complaints:

- Identify how you currently handle complaints.

- Get your staff to help work out how you'll handle complaints, and who will do it.

- Talk about the common complaints you might receive and role-play ways to solve them.

- Write it all down.

- Train your staff on how they can resolve complaints.

- Let your customers know you're happy to listen to their complaints.

- Record all complaints and responses.

- Give your complaints process a test run and listen to customer and staff feedback. Look to continually improve your complaints process.

Source: Queensland Office of Fair Trading <www.fairtrading.qld.gov.au/handling-complaints.htm>.

Intellectual property

This area of the law covers anything that relates to the confidential information that was used to create or continues to drive your small business. Under intellectual property (IP), you'll find laws relating to areas such as patents, trademarks, copyright, designs and plant breeder's rights. The creative stuff. IP Australia is the Australian Government agency in charge of all areas of intellectual property. 'In business terms, this means your proprietary knowledge — a key component of success in business today', states the IP website. You have to register all forms of intellectual property with IP Australia if you want it protected, except circuit layout rights and copyright (see the *Copyright Act 1968*), which are both automatically covered. For comprehensive information on all aspects of intellectual property, go to:

→ IP Australia's Smart Start site <www.ipaustralia.gov.au/ smartstart/>, which has information specifically for anyone starting a new business or buying an existing small business.

→ IP Australia also has a site called IP Toolbox <www.iptoolbox.gov.au>, which goes into more detail about the management of your intellectual property.

Product safety

Consumers should be able to expect that every product they buy is safe to be used or consumed. According to <www.business.gov.au>, safe products are ones that 'meet relevant safety standards, provide clear instructions for proper use and include warnings against possible misuse'. Children's toys, for example, have strict, national stipulations in relation to safety (no small bits for tiny tots). There are mandatory product safety standards that you, as a business owner, have to comply with. These are outlined in the Trade Practices Act, and enforced by the ACCC. The ACCC stipulates that 'all suppliers — including manufacturers, importers, distributors, hirers and retailers — are responsible for ensuring that goods they supply comply with the relevant mandatory standards'. To make sure your business complies with the product safety regulations, visit the product safety part of the ACCC's website (find it under 'For Businesses'). You can search for your particular product type, or get a raft of general information.

Warranties and refunds

Good business is about looking after your customers. If they're not happy with the goods or services they buy from you, they can complain to the ACCC under the guidelines of the *Trade Practices Act 1974*. All complaints are taken seriously and, if upheld, can result in fines to your business.

To receive a refund for a product, customers need a valid receipt. Be aware of your warranty and refund responsibilities under the Act by first going to the ACCC website <www.accc.gov.au>, which offers stacks of information on the rights of consumers and your obligations. It offers a free booklet, *Warranties and Refunds: a guide for consumers and business*, which is available online (go to 'Publications', then 'For Businesses', click on 'Dealing with Customers' and then the 'Warranty and refund obligations' link at the bottom of the page). Plus, it has an online video that specifically outlines your business's rights and obligations under warranty and refund laws.

State and territory governments also have jurisdiction over warranty and refund legislation. So check with your closest fair trading authority (you'll find a list on <www.business.gov.au>).

Question: *How do I resolve disputes and protect my small business legally?*

Answer: *Having a grasp of a few important legal areas will help you stay out of strife.*

You deal with people every day, whether they're your customers, your employees or your suppliers. Federal and state and territory laws stipulate that these dealings are fair and reasonable, and that everyone has their rights respected. As a small business owner it's part of the gig to know a little bit about a lot, and this includes some of the laws relating to protecting people. You don't need a law degree; just having an idea about some areas of the law that are relevant to your business is usually enough. Then, if any situation does flare up into a legal stoush, you'll at least be able to understand some of the jargon that gets tossed around by legal professionals in any claim for compensation. This bit of knowledge could just save you time, and money.

Debt recovery

Keeping your cash flow on track is hard enough, let alone when someone doesn't pay you for the goods or services you supply them with. Bad debts are the bane of small business, costing you and causing you stress you don't need. Having an idea of what you can do within the law to recover your money can help. First, you're expected to have made every effort to talk to the person or company that owes you and ask them to honour the sale. If this fails, you can try writing a letter of demand. This is supposed to remind your debtor, in writing, that you need to be paid, by a certain date. Say in the letter that if they don't pay by then, you'll be starting legal action. Be careful what you write: you're not allowed to threaten or harass them in the letter. You can ask your solicitor to draw up a letter of demand, or you can get a free sample from the Arts Law Centre of Australia <www.artslaw.com.au/LegalInformation>.

A letter of demand has two purposes, the Arts Law Centre states. 'First, it warns the debtor of your intention to commence legal proceedings unless payment is made and gives the debtor one more opportunity to pay. Secondly, the letter is a document which may be tendered in evidence during court proceedings as written proof of your claim of the debt owed and your attempt to settle the matter.' If you don't get a response from your letter of demand, you can send a more formal version, called a statutory demand. But if you're going down this more formal legal track, it's a good idea to talk to your lawyer or solicitor to get his or her advice first (if you don't have one, go to question 7 for tips on finding a good one).

Discrimination

Discrimination doesn't have to hit you in the face. It can be subtle. Which is why knowing a bit about the parameters of this legal minefield is worthwhile for small business owners. That way you can make sure that everything in your business is aimed the other way. According to <www.workplace.gov.au>, discrimination can be direct ('treating one person less favourably than another because of particular attributes, such as race, colour, sex, sexual preference, age, disability, medical record, impairment, marital status, pregnancy, potential pregnancy, family responsibilities, criminal record, trade union activity, political opinion, religion, national extraction or social origin') or indirect ('treating everyone the same but in a way that ends up being unfair to a specific group of people. An example of this is where the design of a workplace prevents a person with a disability from accessing the equipment needed to do the job'). There are federal and state and territory anti-discrimination legislations; the Human Rights and Equal Opportunity Commission <www.hreoc. gov.au> administers the federal realm. Its website includes every type of discrimination that's relevant to small business (including 'vicarious liability', which is when all reasonable steps have been implemented in your workplace to limit your liability). To make sure your business does toe the line in this area of the law, the commission also recommends that you put together some sort of discrimination and harassment policy, particularly sexual harassment. If you don't have any idea of how to do this, there are fact sheets on the Human Rights Commission website to get you started.

Dispute resolution

Sometimes commonsense doesn't prevail, no matter how hard you try, and disputes arise. Whether it's a dispute with a customer or a supplier, the ideal outcome is to be able to smooth over the dispute professionally but informally.

'Alternative dispute resolution is usually a much cheaper alternative and disputes are often resolved much quicker than progressing through the courts, which can take years', states the Department of Innovation, Industry, Science and Research's dedicated small business legal issues website (visit <http://sblegal.innovation.gov.au> — it gives you legal defin- itions and links to 1500 other law sites so it's a must-look). 'As a result, alternative dispute resolution, or ADR as it is often referred to, is becoming a popular method of dealing with disputes and is being encouraged by the government.' Under the banner of ADR, you'll find 'mediation, arbitration, conciliation and counselling'.

To make these dispute resolution tools effective and impartial, you'll need a third party to be part of the process, if you're doing it yourself. Your nearest Business Enterprise Centre can help, plus there are some handy hints on solving any disputes with customers on the BEC Australia website <www.beca.org.au>. You can also get information from your state or territory's fair trading agency (see question 40 for contact details).

Employee awards

Employee awards count in the eyes of the law. The terms of minimum pay, maximum working hours, holiday and sick leave entitlements and long service leave, among other things, are covered under most state and federal awards. The website <www.business.gov.au> has links to the awards and agreements in every state and territory. You should also go to the Australian Government's Fair Work Online website <www.fairwork.gov.au>, which includes comprehensive infor- mation about the general legal expectations of you as an employer when it comes to how you pay and treat your staff. Plus, there's a 'tools and templates' section specifically for small business owners. So much to know: but it's worth it!

Action item: spotting a scam

Small businesses are sometimes the target of scams that can cost thousands of dollars. You don't want to be one of them. That's why the Australian Competition and Consumer Commission has created *The Little Book of Scams* (find it under 'Publications' on the ACCC website). According to the ACCC, the 'scams, swindles, rorts and rip-offs' that can damage small business include unscrupulous employment and investment opportunities, and online banking scams. You should also check out the Australian Securities & Investments Commission's Fido website <www.fido.gov.au>. There's a huge section on scams and warnings: how to spot them and the laws that protect you.

42 Question: *What do I need to know about e-security?*

Answer: *Be vigilant with everything your business does online.*

Internet security is always a hot topic for small business. You can imagine the damage a scam email or computer virus could do to your system. You could lose your payroll and business details, including your customer database and future orders. Disaster. The same holds for your business finances. If fraudsters ever got access to your funds, it could spell the end of your success.

A national survey by the Australian Institute of Criminology (AIC) found that computer security breaches affected 13 per cent of Australian small businesses in 2007. The most common incidents involved viruses and malicious code attacks (also known as worms, which aim to get into and destroy multi-computer systems), and in 40 per cent of cases computer hardware or software was corrupted. In this survey the average cost to small business was $360. They were let off relatively lightly when you consider that, according to the AIC, computer security incidents cost medium-sized businesses an average $2757, and large business suffered average losses of $17 578.

In another survey, the AIC found that a third of online traders have been a victim of online fraud (with average losses from $100 to $3500), and over half of those businesses were repeatedly targeted. Internet banking fraud, phishing (when you're tricked into giving your personal or banking and finance details which are then used to tap into your bank accounts) and email scams have become even bigger business since these statistics were released. Now, internet fraud costs businesses globally billions every year. The way to thwart them is to be vigilant with everything your business does online, including finances and external orders. Putting some of the following strategies in place won't protect you totally, but they will make it harder for cyber crime to hit your business.

Install a firewall

According to the Australian Communications and Media Authority <www.acma.gov.au>, firewalls broadly aim to block any type of internet traffic other than what you say should be allowed. A firewall should stop intruders who attempt to remotely browse your files, or spyware from 'phoning home' with your private information. It's your first line of defence against intruders. Most recent versions of Windows operating systems come with a firewall, or you can buy firewalls and antivirus software online or at your local computer store.

Update antivirus software

It pays to remember that cyber criminals are always trying to create viruses that get around current versions of antivirus software, and jump over firewalls. Update your system with the latest versions of antivirus software every few months, from companies such as Norton Antivirus. And if you're sent notification of an automatic update, make sure you install it straight away. The Australian Government's Stay Smart Online initiative at <www.staysmartonline.gov.au> also has a free 'E-security Alert Service' that informs you of the latest security risks and offers fact sheets on how to protect your business from online threats (go to 'Small Business e-security' and then click on the 'E-security Alert Service' link to sign up for the service).

Action item: e-commerce checklist

The Treasury has comprehensive information about e-security on its website <www.treasury. gov.au>, including a handy e-commerce checklist for small business. Even if you're not yet offering your services or products online, you might one day. This site will help you get there.

Secure your payments

If your customers buy products from your website, make sure they know (it has to be obvious) how you're going to secure their payment (credit card) details. Secure sites use encryption methods to transfer data across the internet. All customer details are basically scrambled so that they can't be picked up and deciphered by intruders. Make this a priority if you are setting up an online store. Once you have a secure e-commerce site (get your web designer to make it happen), you should display the secure site symbol (a padlock) on your web pages. If you're just setting up your website, be aware of the e-commerce capabilities, such as secure connections to banks, price transparency for any extra bank charges you pass on to the consumer and reputable payment gateways such as PayPal, that you will need. (And make sure you've read question 29!)

Watch what you do online

When you're accessing your business banking, you should always login by typing your bank's web address into the address bar on your computer. This guarantees that you are going straight to your bank's site. Never go to your bank through a link that's been emailed to you, as it's probably one of the many dummy sites that are set up by cyber criminals to get your login details and then fleece you of funds. Also, you should never respond to a link that's sent to you claiming it's from your bank: they're the domain of hoax emails. If your bank wants to contact you, they won't do it through email.

Know your limits

The website Protect Your Financial Identity <www.protect financialid.org.au>, which has been put together by the Australian Bankers' Association, Australian High Tech Crime Centre and the Australian Securities & Investments Commission, suggests that you don't have a huge limit for the credit card that's attached to your bank account. 'Also consider whether it may be safer to use a separate credit card account for online transactions and when you are overseas', the site advises. Always know your credit limit and keep a close eye on your account balances. The moment you spot something that doesn't look right, contact your bank.

Use passwords that are difficult to guess

The more complicated the passwords on your computer, email accounts and online banking facilities, the harder it will be for criminals to work them out. According to the Australian Computer Emergency Response Team (AusCERT), all of your passwords should be at least eight characters long and a mix-ture of cases, punctuation and digits. It offers some other tips on choosing good passwords; its site at <www.auscert.org.au> is definitely worth a look if you're interested in further protecting your business finances from cyber crime.

Don't store all your information in the one spot

Back up, back up, back up should be every small business owner's mantra. If you don't back up your computer system every day, you could lose valuable information, let alone open yourself up for disaster if your computer is accessed in some way. And don't keep your backup files in the same spot as your computer.

Don't open the door to strangers

Never open emails and attachments from companies or people you don't know. If you are wondering whether an email is suspect, go to the Australian Competition and Consumer Commission's SCAMwatch site <www.scamwatch.gov.au> for more information or to report it. By being aware in all your business's online activities you'll certainly reduce your risks.

Part VI

Growing, growing, gone?

This section aims to help you get the most out of the highs, minimise the lows and maintain the spark that propelled you into business for yourself in the first place.

As a wise owner, you should always have your finger on your business's pulse. Can you sustain the momentum, both professionally and personally? What about when you don't want to do it any more: have you set up a financially successful exit strategy? As you'll see here, it's never too early to have these conversations so that you make the most of your small business adventure.

43 **Question:** *Business is going gang busters: when is the best time to expand?*

Answer: *When you've really considered what bigger means for your business.*

Bigger is better. Somehow this has become the accepted measure of small business success. If you're going really well, you're growing. If you're not growing, you must be doing something wrong. Just remember that success is absolutely in the eyes of the beholder. And while the mythical Land of Opportunity is an exciting, inspiring place, it's often not all it's cracked up to be. So be prepared. If your business is going gang busters and you're looking to expand, it could be a wilder adventure than you ever imagined.

When the time's right

There are lots of different ways the business world measures success. And it varies from industry to industry. You might rate success in terms of size. You've built your business from nothing, and now you're about to employ another 10 people. Wow, you must be doing well. Or maybe your order book is bulging: surely you're successful because everyone wants your product or service. Just be aware that a growing business isn't always a successful business. 'If you're wanting to get bigger, make sure it is the best outcome for your business', says Dr Graham Godbee of the Macquarie Graduate School of Management. Think about it before you do it. 'Then, if you decide the time is right, make the growth sensible and controlled.' Godbee says there can be better times in your business cycle to expand than others. 'If you get too much bigger at certain points, it can be a big jump. Sometimes it's better to consolidate rather than grow; however, very few businesses take the time to do this.' (See the sustainable growth formula in question 32 to calculate your big jump moments.)

Different types of expansion

If you're set on expanding your business, you have to work out the sort of growth you want. 'Amazingly, many businesses view sales growth or some similar measure (like market share) as the growth goal', Godbee writes in his book *Manage for All Seasons*. 'Ideally, it should be profit or sustainability or something more "bottom line" than just sales.' He thinks there are essentially four different ways to expand your business: spend the time and really nut out which tack you should take.

→ *Market penetration.* This is when you either grow the volume within your current market or snare market share off competitors. This strategy can work if your business has a small share of the market. 'Going from 4 per cent market share to 6 per cent market share in a static market would effectively increase the sales of the business by 50 per cent', Godbee says.

→ *Product development.* You develop new products to sell to your existing market. Maybe you start cross-selling another service. Be aware that your competitors might sniff what you're doing and do the same or, as he points out, 'you could find businesses from other industries now targeting your traditional customers'.

→ *Market development.* You take your existing product or service to new markets. These markets are either geographic (regions or countries) or demographic (types of customers in your existing region), notes Godbee. 'If there is a want for your product or service that is not being currently met in other markets, then such a strategy should be very reasonable. Otherwise, you will need to enter the market with little knowledge of the customers and take market share from established locals — not easy!' You should start any market research by going to the Australian Bureau of Statistics website <www.abs.gov.au>, which has a mountain of information about people and their living and purchasing habits.

→ *Diversification*. This is selling products and services you've never dealt with and that are unfamiliar to your customers. 'There are examples of success but they are rare and usually required considerable luck', Godbee says. 'However, if your existing products and services are at the end of their product life cycle or your market is shrinking, you may need to consider a radical diversification move. Examples include modem manufacturers changing to become mining companies.'

Go back to your goals

What was it that made you set up your business in the first place? What goals did you write down? How does expanding your business in any of the above ways fit in with these goals? If one of your aims of setting up your small business was to have more free time, does going even more gang busters achieve this? 'You should also be asking how it is going to affect the foundations of your business', says Kathryn Conder, partner of executive and business mentoring firm Carnegie Management Group. What are the cracks that are going to open up? 'If you have a one-storey house and add another storey before the foundations are in good order ... It's one of the biggest mistakes that small businesses make.'

Plan your move

Don't expand your business without a concrete plan. Go through all the 'what ifs'. How do you hope to ask your staff to work longer or harder, without knowing where it fits in to your business's goals (which you've hopefully shared with them since day one)? 'By taking on a new team member or new premises, what implications will that have for your business?' asks Conder. She advises her clients to ask lots of questions of themselves, and write down the answers. Exactly how is your business going to expand (logistically)? And what sort of knowledge and skills do you need to make it happen without having an impact on what you currently do, particularly on your standards of customer service? Are you going to be able to find the right people to do the extra work? And are you prepared to change the way you do things, as the boss, in order to make the expansion a success?

Capital needs

You're going to need some sort of capital injection to expand. Again, this will totally depend on the business you're in, but you'll possibly move to a bigger building, get more computers for the staff you'll hire, buy or hire extra vehicles, have more stock on hand, and ramp up the capacity of your production or service offering. Have you thought about the tax implications of your plans? As it states on <www.business.gov.au>: 'Higher turnover means more tax. You will also need to register for GST if your growth means your turnover now exceeds $75 000 (see more on taxes in question 11).' Then there are the extra resources you're going to need, and how you'll make this happen. 'Companies that expand successfully have done the planning and are prepared to work hard', adds Conder. 'If you haven't spent the time forecasting and costing your plan, and considering the whole process, don't grow.'

Other things to consider

As well as thinking about all the direct business implications of expansion, the Australian Government <www. business.gov.au> suggests that you also look at:

- *Your recordkeeping capabilities.* Are your business systems capable of accurately keeping more records, particularly for things with legal obligations for your business, such as your tax and payroll obligations?

The Australian Taxation Office has a lot of information that will help you keep your recordkeeping in step with your expansion <www.ato.gov.au>.

▫ *Any privacy implications.* Businesses with an annual turnover of more than $3 million have to comply with the *Privacy Act 1988* when it comes to how you handle any customers' personal information. For the lowdown on the privacy obligations relevant to your business, contact the Office of the Privacy Commissioner <www.privacy.gov.au> or phone 1300 363 992.

▫ *Extra licences and permits.* 'Expanding your service or diversifying your products could mean your business needs to comply with additional licences or permits', states <www.business.gov.au>. The Business Licence Information Service (BLIS) in your state or territory has more information on what you might need (access your nearest BLIS via the online directory at <www.business.gov.au/directory>). You should also check out any relevant planning and zoning regulations with your local council, as these could also impact your growth plans.

44 **Question:** *How much money should I throw into growing my business?*

Answer: *It really depends on why you want to grow.*

Opportunities come up all the time. Deciding which ones to invest in and which ones to leave alone is vital for the sustainability of your small business. Hopefully, the growth you go for is based on something solid, not just a hunch.

You've spent the time planning your expansion (after reading question 43!). But then comes the million-dollar question: how much money do you need to plough into this growth, and where will it come from? Capital raising is one of the reasons small business expansion plans often come undone. You didn't think your growth strategy would cost *that* much. Remember, sometimes the idea of growing your business is more attractive than the reality. Going with your gut is fine. But carefully weighing up all the considerations in an overall plan is the smarter thing to do.

Your rationale for growing

Ask yourself again: why do you want to grow your business? 'A lot of growth doesn't help your business', says Dr Graham Godbee of the Macquarie Graduate School of Management. Instead it confuses things. Suddenly, what was running well isn't enough. You need extra people, different skills, more robust systems, and even bigger premises to make it all happen. 'You have to have a big-picture plan and then ask yourself if you have the skills and resources to make this plan happen', he cautions. Do you want to grow fast or slowly? What does this mean in terms of a time frame? And how will your existing activities support the plan?

Find this out by doing an accurate forecast and costings. This could be something you've already done in a business plan (from question 6). The Victorian Department of Innovation, Industry and Regional Development's online business portal <www.business.vic.gov.au> offers a free cash flow forecast and break even point information sheet. This is very user friendly and will really help you extrapolate your cash flow to see what your growth goals are actually going to cost your business. It's a great way to see if your growth plans are viable, and whether or not you'll need to investigate funding options.

Action item: online checklist

The Australian Government has set up a Growing Your Business Checklist at <www.business.gov. au>. It poses all the questions to think about before you launch into growing your business, and the government agencies that can help you in your quest. Definitely worth a look before you leap.

Keep it simple

When it comes to funding any growth, the best idea in business is always to use your own money. 'Financially, you shouldn't need more money to facilitate continued growth', says Godbee. 'It should be able to be supported by the business. If you're profitable, you can use a lot of retained earnings to do it.' That way, you'll only grow by as much as you can afford. If you've always put a percentage of net profits back into the business, you might have some savings you could use. But will it be enough? The last thing you want to do is to start growing, and end up in a downward cash flow spiral because you can't continue to pay for the expansion. In this case, try talking to your bank about workable strategies.

You can use some debt for growth, as long as you get a return on the debt and can service it with cash flow, says Godbee. 'Stable cash flows would allow higher debt levels than more volatile or variable cash flows.' For finance options, see the breakout box on p. 206. If you do approach your bank or financial institution, be prepared. Have your business plan well and truly mapped out. Show the bank you've thought about the growth, and have the forecasts to prove how good it's going to be.

Financing growth

These are the finance options the Australian Government suggests you consider for your business growth. Just be aware of what each one could cost you in the long run.

- ❑ Loans: from a bank or financial institution.

- ❑ Savings: from your own bank account.

- ❑ Business angels: private investors who come in and share their knowledge and expertise for a share of the business (see <www.businessangels.com.au>).

- ❑ Venture capitalists: investors focused solely on the new ideas and growth potential and how to make this happen (which could include cutting costs), in return for finance.

- ❑ Share ownership or equity: when you split the ownership of your business (and share of the profits) for a certain investment. You can also make share ownership offerings to your employees. Just get it all written down in legal documents by your solicitor.

- ❑ Floating on the stock exchange: you can float your company on the stock market, selling shares to the public to raise finance. Don't go into this lightly as there are lots of legal and disclosure demands on publicly listed companies.

- ❑ Government funding: the three levels of Australian government—federal, state and local—have funding and incentive schemes that you can tap into, particularly if your growth plans are in the areas of 'research and development, innovation and exporting'.

Source: <www.business.gov.au>.

Other options

'Sometimes you can ask your suppliers for better terms', suggests Godbee. 'Some businesses even get suppliers to put money into their business.' This all makes business sense: you're leveraging off your existing relationships to facilitate your bigger, brighter future. Just make sure the relationships are rock solid before you go down this road. Seriously think about whether you want to grow using other people's money, particularly family and friends (remember question 17?).

Maybe you think it's time to take on a partner. Just find out if this person is going to be a passive investor, or if he or she has management capabilities you could use in your business. 'Whatever outside investment you consider, it's essential that you have a shareholders' agreement', says Godbee. Get it all written down so that everyone knows where they stand.

Take your time

Building a successful small business takes time. And the reality, in all but the luckiest of cases, is that you won't be a millionaire in a month. So why should you expect your business to grow overnight just because you're throwing extra cash at it? Spend the time to really plan your expansion. It might take you a couple of months to crunch all the numbers, but it will be time well spent in the end when your business grows in a way you can control.

'Good strategy requires us to understand what is happening around us and the direction in which your business is heading', writes Godbee in his book *Manage for All Seasons*. 'We also need to know what our business has going for it and where it may have deficiencies.' Here, he suggests utilising your SWOT analysis (the one you did from question 6). It will show you in black and white the strengths you should be bolstering, the weaknesses and threats you need to be mindful of and the most obvious opportunities for your business.

Adds Godbee: 'The steps sound simple, but the thought processes are complex and require a holistic view of the external and internal environments.' Put it all into a strategy that you can tell your team (or investors) about. After all, your people and internal processes will be there long after the extra funds go in and out of your bank account. So make them a lynchpin in your growth goals.

45 Question: *I'm thinking about export: what do I need to know before I go?*

Answer: *The simplest export opportunity still needs a strategy.*

Snaring an export deal is another milestone of small business success. But international opportunities also come with risks; financially and logistically. So don't jump into exporting before you've sorted out a solid strategy. The information you'll find in this section is just the tip of the iceberg. There are several federal, state and territory government authorities that have more advice (see the 'who can you call' list in the breakout box, p. 209). If you're even slightly considering export, the best place to start your information gathering is the Australian Government's trade commission, Austrade. Its website <www. austrade.gov.au> has a tonne of export information and contact details so you can ask questions of its experts.

Doing your research

The more research you do, and the more organised you are, the more successful your export experience will be. 'Companies that do well at home can generally export', states Austrade. However, it's often a different world to do business in, so spend the time learning about foreign markets and your readiness for the plunge. Market research is the key. Cover the same sorts of things you did before you launched your products or services locally: identify your market and the growth prospects, and examine your competition (see more market research tips in question 27). Then there are the export-specific things to sort out, such as any international regulations, duties and cultural factors, as well as logistics and freight constraints.

Use internet search engines such as Google to collect general information about your potential overseas market. For more specific details, utilise Austrade's expertise. It often runs seminars specifically on doing business in different countries (for details call 13 28 78), with tips on what's acceptable business behaviour. Then drill down to information that relates to your particular product or service. Why would overseas customers buy it? Austrade can help you with this too (some of its advice is free). For specific published reports on different markets, contact Austrade or some of the private market research companies listed on the Austrade site.

Action item: who can you call?

- Austrade export advisers: phone 13 28 78 or online at <www.austrade.gov.au>. For information on Austrade export workshops, go to <www.austrade.gov.au/trade-events/default.aspx>.

- The Export Finance and Insurance Corporation (EFIC): phone 1800 887 588 or online at <www.efic.gov.au>.

- Australian Customs Service: phone 1300 363 263 or online at <www.customs.gov.au>.

- Austrade's online division: if you're thinking of exporting through your website, contact <www.exportingonline.gov.au>.

Action item *(cont'd)*: who can you call?

□ The Australian Chamber of Commerce and Industry (ACCI) <www.acci.asn.au> or the Australian Industry Group <www.aigroup.asn.au> can help you with networking opportunities.

Put it into a plan

The Australian Government suggests on <www.business. gov.au> that your export plan should include information on target markets, time frames (for production and delivery), customs duties and any overseas marketing strategies. Like your business plan, it's okay to keep it simple. Just going through the process of thinking about how export could affect your business will help you focus. What do you hope to achieve from taking your product or service overseas? Write down your specific goals. 'Particular aims could include reducing seasonal demand swings, reducing fixed costs, fully realising production capacity, accessing new technology, consolidating your international reputation or matching the performance of your domestic competitors who are already selling offshore', states Austrade. Bring every decision back to those goals.

Once you start getting all your thoughts, and the information you've found, on paper, it'll help you focus on the next steps. Think about your export price (it might be different to your domestic price), volumes and what your capacity will be and a delivery schedule (ask a shipping agent — you'll find them in the *Yellow Pages*), Austrade suggests. Make sure your production is up to the task so that you can guarantee time frames.

Seize the day

Sometimes export opportunities land in your lap. Your products or services might have been noticed online (the internet is such an international showcase), or maybe an industry association or a business associate has been approached by oversees companies, and your brand was mentioned. Then again, you may have already got your business listed on Austrade's Australian Suppliers Directory <www.austrade.gov.au/asd>. Whichever way it comes, your first international sales enquiry is something to get excited about. Just stay in control.

Make sure you understand everything that's said in an export discussion with potential customers (if you don't get the language, get an interpreter). Check the customer's credentials and whether they're talking about a one-off deal or something more long term. Austrade's export advisers can help you do all this. Take the time to decide if the opportunity is right for your business. Really nut out the logistics of the deal. Get the advice of a good customs broker and freight forwarder or shipping agent (Austrade has some contact details on its site under 'About Exporting') to help you work through all the documentation as well as find you the cheapest and fastest ways to ship your goods. And before you sign an international sales contract, get some solid legal advice from a solicitor or lawyer with international contract experience.

What's it cost?

Costs will depend on your type of business and which countries you're aiming to export to. It might cost you thousands of dollars to set up your distribution channels well. There are insurance and customs costs to factor in (a customs broker can help you work this out — you can find them in the *Yellow Pages*). You'll need a marketing budget so customers overseas know about you. By using the internet as a marketing tool (see question 29 for tips), Austrade says you can reduce your marketing spend; however, you still might need to do something on the ground. The use of e-commerce (including electronic transactions) can also reduce some of your transaction costs. Add it all up.

There's credit insurance to factor in, which Austrade strongly advises you get to 'protect your cash flow from payment default and customer insolvency'. And because you're probably dealing in foreign currency payments, have an idea of the impact of what it means to your margins when the Aussie dollar (and other currencies) goes up and down in value. You could investigate opening a foreign currency account for your overseas payments. That way you can charge (and refund if you have to) a US customer in US dollars, a European customer in euros and a British customer in pounds. As well as protecting you from yo-yoing currencies (you get to choose when you convert US dollars into Australian dollars and you can compare forex companies for the best rate), it gives you credibility in foreign markets.

It can be a lot to consider, so it pays to get some advice. Book an appointment with your bank manager and your accountant to make sure the whole thing is a realistic option, considering your cash flow forecasts and any currency fluctuations. And call Austrade — its export advisers are a worthwhile first port of call. They'll be able to tell you if you can apply for financial export assistance, known as the Export Market Development Grant (EMDG) scheme. This aims to help you with some of the costs of opening your business up to the world. If you qualify for assistance, the Australian Government will reimburse you for up to 50 per cent of your eligible export expenses if they are more than $10 000 over two years. To score this funding, you'll have to supply Austrade with relevant financial statements and other information about your business. So get sorted early on.

The ins and outs of importing

Just like exporting, there are a stack of regulations and laws you need to get your head around if you're interested in importing. According to Sensis's *Small Business, Big*

Opportunity, 45 per cent of exporters also import, so you might already have an idea of some of the customs and logistics issues, such as freight. If you're just starting your investigations into the world of importing, it pays to get up close and personal with all the laws that will affect your business. The Australian Government has some general information at <www.business.gov.au>. If you're serious, spend time on the Australian and Customs Border Protection Service (Customs) website: <www.customs.gov.au>. Here are a few importing tips to start you off.

- *Know your market.* As with exporting, you need to do your market research to make sure you're importing for the right reasons (if your customers aren't interested, why bother?). You might have spotted a cost advantage, or unique products your customers can't get in Australia: if you know that's what they want, you'll be in a safer spot to go for it.

- *Know the laws.* There are customs, permits, duties and import regulations. Most of them are enforced by Customs. Do your homework by contacting Customs on 1300 363 263 or online. It also can tell you if your business is eligible for import assistance. As well, the Australian Government has labelling requirements for goods imported into Australia. The Australian Competition and Consumer Commission (ACCC) has all these details on its website (go to <www.accc. gov.au> and click on 'For businesses' then 'product safety and labelling').

- *Know the quarantine requirements.* Some goods are held up in customs because they need to be inspected and treated, or even quarantined for a period of time, before coming into the country. Put this into your time frames. Contact the Australian

The ins and outs of importing *(cont'd)*

Quarantine and Inspection Service (AQIS) on
<www.aqis.gov.au> or call 1800 020 504.

□ *Know the culture.* Importers who do well are
often on a plane, forming solid relationships with
their suppliers (learning the language helps) and
securing the on-time delivery of the goods. Get your
passport ready!

46 **Question:** *Is franchising an option that I should consider?*

Answer: *To buy or create a franchise, you need to put in a lot of groundwork.*

Relationships, systems and a proven formula. They're three reasons people are keen to buy into a small business franchise. The relationship is with the franchisor: the person with the original business idea who has the expertise to guide you (at a price) along the path to success. The systems are the how-tos of doing their business, including management, marketing, training and merchandising processes. The proven formula is the runs on the board. Do as they've done and you'll undoubtedly do well. But is it that easy? And what about trying to franchise an original business idea: what do you need to do to make it happen?

Franchise facts

You'll find different types of franchises in every industry sector. The most popular franchises are known as business format franchises (for example, retailers who share their brand and systems to other retailers). There are also product franchises (for example, new car dealerships) and trademark franchises (for example, licensing the distribution of a soft drink brand). The Franchise Council of Australia <www.franchise.org.au> estimates that the number of franchises grew by 14.6 per cent (net growth) between 2006 and 2008, and 28 franchises appeared in the 2008 *BRW* List of Top 500 Private Companies in Australia. The secret of their success is simple: they have created strong and distinctive brands underpinned by water-tight management systems that can be replicated anywhere.

The highest performing franchisees (individual owners), according to the Franchise Council, are the ones who totally believe in the business systems they've bought into. They do everything 'by the book'. They don't try to reinvent the wheel. Instead, they focus on 'generating value, rather than volume, of business', states the Council. 'They also achieve higher rates of cross-selling ("Would you like fries with that?")'. While buying into a franchise means you'll be your own small business boss, you should always be aware that you're expected to run it within the boundaries set by the franchisor.

Franchise seminars

The Franchise Council of Australia holds information seminars (some cost as little as $25) around Australia for people looking to buy into a franchise or create one off the back of their business's success. You get to ask questions of a franchisor, franchisee and ACCC and state government representatives. Call 1300 669 030. The Council also offers free information brochures on all aspects of franchising which you can download from its website <www.franchise.org.au>.

Getting into one

There's a huge list of franchises on the Franchise Council website <www.franchisebusiness.com.au>, or call it on

1300 669 030. But before you go through the list, ask yourself why you want to get into a franchise in the first place. Define your personal and professional goals for the business. It'll help you match yourself to the right sort of franchise. Think of it as a marriage. Like any union, it'll be more successful if you know a lot about your prospective partner before you commit. The way to make it a win–win for both of you in the relationship, states the Franchise Council, is to appreciate the trade-off that happens: the cost-effective expansion benefits to the franchisor's brand; and the low-risk systems that the franchisee gets the use of to make their own money.

Before you commit to a franchise, the Council advises you to get as much information as you can about the general process and a couple of particular franchises. Contact each franchisor and ask for an application pack. They should be keen to help. Make sure the application pack includes all the facts you'll need to make an informed decision (including the exact sign-up and operating costs, and the benefits to both parties). However, don't make any decisions until you've spoken to an adviser (an accountant or lawyer) with specialised experience in the area of franchising (go to the Franchise Council's website for a list of qualified advisers). The 'marriage' is legally binding under the terms of a franchise agreement (each one can be different). Each agreement has to comply with the mandatory Franchising Code of Conduct, which is enforced by the Australian Competition and Consumer Commission (ACCC). You can view the Code of Conduct via the Franchise Council site or through the ACCC site <www.accc.gov.au>. Have an expert go through the code and the commercial contract with you so you're fully aware of your obligations and responsibilities before going any further.

The cost

The cost of buying into a franchise can vary. The Franchise Council says you can expect to pay anything from $5000 to more than $1 million, which covers your up-front franchise fees and set-up costs. Retail franchises can cost from $50000 to more than $250000 (the shop fittings and stock may or may not be included). On top of these costs you'll pay either ongoing fixed fees or a percentage of turnover fees (royalties) for all the support systems and any group marketing activities. 'Fixed monthly amounts may range from $50 per month up, while percentage fees may range from 2 per cent to as much as 15 per cent', states the Council.

Find out what you'll be getting for the money. Go through all the financials with your accountant or, better still, an accountant with franchising experience, and work out how much working capital you'll need to pay for the initial set-up and ongoing costs. Your bank might even offer specialised franchise business loans, so it's worth checking with it too. In all your purchasing investigations, be aware that the Franchising Code of Conduct has specific rules when it comes to purchase cooling-off periods. Check the details and collect as much information as you can.

Setting one up yourself

'Some of today's largest businesses have used franchising to finance and accelerate their growth into world brands', states the Franchise Council. But don't look at franchising as the easy way to expand your business. It's not. In fact, the process of getting your business ready to franchise can cost thousands of dollars (after you get all the legal documentation sorted) and take a few years, and then it can be a few years after this before any net profits start rolling in. This is why it's vital you know exactly what you want to achieve as the franchisor. Then start your planning.

The Franchise Council says that a franchise-ready business should 'be successful, distinctive and replicable'. It should have a proven track record. It also needs well-implemented management systems, from admin and finance to training, marketing and customer service, which could be replicated by anyone else. If you go down the franchising path, you'll need to write a comprehensive operations manual for all of your franchisees to follow. If they'd have trouble getting everything right, you'll have to go back to the drawing board. Australia's Franchising Code of Conduct doesn't give you any room to make errors, and you are obliged to fully disclose all relevant details of your business model to prospective franchisees. Any complaints against a franchisor will be investigated by the ACCC.

Not every small business will be right for a franchise. But if you believe yours has the potential, you should commit the time to set everything up properly and pay the money to get qualified legal and financial advice. Only then will you be in the right spot to find the right franchisees. It's a relationship you'll really want to work. After all, everything they do will reflect on your brand. A franchisee who happily buys into your systems is more likely to succeed. And their success will make you money. So make them a prime consideration in your expansion plans.

 Question: *I get on well with my customers: should I mix business with pleasure?*

Answer: *Just always keep your business in mind.*

Golf games and sailing days, tickets to the footy, charity lunches: a lot of business has always been done out of the office. These social events can create warm and fuzzy feelings about your business with clients and potential customers. They also can be a recipe for disaster if you don't handle the situation, and yourself, well. Getting on with your customers isn't enough. You have to know how to walk the business-vs-pleasure tightrope when you invite them out socially. Remember, it all still comes back to your business, and making these relationships work for you.

Know your goals

The decision to socialise with customers and clients shouldn't be taken lightly. Friendships can come and go, but you don't want your business relationships to suffer as a result. If you want new friends, it's often wise to go and find them outside your business circle. However, Associate Professor Isabel Metz, of Melbourne Business School, says it really does depend on the type of business you're in. 'Compare a pharmacy to a financial planner', she says. 'Socialising with customers is less relevant to a pharmacy and more appropriate for financial planners because it's part of doing business.' She thinks there are some specific goals that you should apply to any socialising event:

→ *To widen your networks*. 'Financial planners, for example, benefit from word-of-mouth referrals and their business is based on trust', she says. 'However, for pharmacists, a lot of their success is about service and location — their business isn't necessarily influenced by referrals.'

→ *To strengthen the business relationship*. 'Pharmacists can do this when they provide the service', says Metz. 'Financial planners also do this when they provide the service. But to strengthen the relationship they may need to mix business with pleasure.'

→ *As a reward for the customer*. Pinpoint who is a good customer and invite this person to a social function. 'This is about the recognition of loyalty', she adds.

Know your customers

You're the one who should know what your customers like and don't like better than anyone. (If you don't, you'd better start some serious market research — see question 27 and come back to this question later!) And you should be using this information for your business's benefit. Look at socialising as a marketing activity, and plan it well. 'Keep in mind that some of your customers will prefer different kinds of social activities to others', says Metz. Knowing these differences is the key. This will allow you to segment your customers based on their values, interests and personalities. Then you can plan an event that will be appreciated by each of the different groups.

This has two benefits: you'll show your customers that you really do understand them, and that you have other clients just like them. 'This relates to the homo-social theory', adds Metz. 'People are more comfortable with people like themselves.' So separate your customers so they're in a group of people they have things in common with. This has the added benefit of a possible networking opportunity for them, too. A win–win.

Action item: corporate gift-giving

Handing out some corporate gifts can tell your customers a lot about your professionalism. Here are some business gift-giving dos and don'ts from <www.wishlist.com.au>:

- Do make it sincere.

- Do think about it well in advance and try to match the gift to the customer.

- Do give a gift that's in good taste.

- Don't give something that's too personal: stay away from anything you'd find in the bathroom or bedroom.

- Don't worry if you miss the moment: you can always send something immediately after a social event. It'll reinforce the good-time feeling your customer came away with.

- Don't give the same gift twice.

- Do your research to make sure your gift-giving is culturally appropriate. 'In some countries gifts are

---

not given until negotiations are completed to avoid the impression that the gift is meant as a bribe. Elsewhere, gifts are exchanged only in private. In some Asian countries, green hats are an insult!', states <www.wishlist.com.au>, which has a list of international gift-giving protocols for different continents on its website.

Source: <www.wishlist.com.au>.

Know yourself

Think about where you feel most comfortable socially and work in a get-together with your customers. However, Metz says it's not a good idea to invite clients to your home. 'Keep it social but not too private', she advises. 'It's good to conduct it in a very public place, such as sporting events. However, avoid situations where you may lose control. Commonsense should prevail.'

Even the most relaxed social interactions with customers will reflect on your business. So go along having thought about how you, as the owner, want the whole event to be perceived. What sort of image of you do you want your customers to go away with? Think about what you'll wear. 'There's always a need for a dress protocol', says Metz. 'Appearance sends a lot of signals to a lot of people, so it pays to be attentive.' If the event happens to be a client end-of-financial-year barbecue in the park, work out how you want the day to unfold: relaxed but still business. Carry this off and it will set the tone of your future interactions with these customers.

Where to draw the line

You get on well with your customers. So it's natural to try enjoying a more social footing with them. However, this doesn't mean they want to be your best friend, or that you should be theirs. Always be on your best behaviour, and control your drinking. On the flipside, you don't want the get-together to be a stitched-up hard sell, either. Enjoy the social time, and let them know how much you appreciate them doing business with you. This is a good way to broach business. Be interested in them, and have some questions up your sleeve about their purchasing habits.

Or you can use the opportunity to make specific business proposals so that they walk away from the event thinking that there actually was something in it for them. Then, know when it's time to wrap it up and go home. It's really not a good look if your customers (or your suppliers and employees for that matter) see you stumbling around at the end of the party. You want your business to be perceived as professional, so follow it through in everything you do.

48 **Question:** *With all this extra work, will my family ever see me?*

Answer: *Getting the right balance really is up to you.*

The hope of achieving a work–life balance could have been one of the reasons you set up your small business in the first place. You'd be in control of your time and, as the boss, you could juggle things so that both your personal and professional lives were fulfilled. You'd have time for family and work. Once you're in the throes of a small business, the reality is often that it's busier than you ever imagined. You end up working harder, and longer, than you ever have. But are you working too much?

It's a very individual thing, says Associate Professor Isabel Metz of the Melbourne Business School, who has researched the area of work–family balance. 'Everyone has a different perspective of what constitutes too much and whether what they do under the work umbrella leaves them satisfied', she says. You might be the sort of person who doesn't worry about working all hours on your business. In fact, you love the thrill. Or you might be at the other end of the personality spectrum, where you've started resenting how much your business is encroaching on the time you have to do other things, such as spending time with your family and friends. Working weekends is just adding to the agony.

Basically, it comes down to how satisfied you are with the peaks and troughs of running your business. Metz suggests you only work the number of hours that keeps you happy with your achievements (both professional and personal). If long hours mean you constantly feel under pressure, it's time to do something about it. 'Research shows lower satisfaction or permanent dissatisfaction with work leads to health consequences, such as fatigue and stress', she says.

Your personality profile

Coping often comes down to your personality type. Type A personalities are assertive, highly goals focused and they tend to be perfectionists. They're the ones who feel compelled to do a lot of things at the same time, very quickly. For Type B personalities, time is more elastic and they tend to be more relaxed about deadlines. 'It's really important to be aware of the type of personality you are so that you can develop strategies to alleviate any potential problems', says Metz. To find out your personality type, you can do a personality test (try an online version based on the works of Jung and the Myers-Briggs Type Indicator at <www.humanmetrics.com>). If your natural tendency is to work to excess, don't wait until something radical happens (Type A personalities tend to be the ones to die of heart attacks) before you attempt to change how you work. Be aware of all the demands on you, and prioritise or get someone in to help if you feel like you're not coping.

Revising your lifestyle

When your business is going well it's easy to want to do it all. But are you putting unnecessary pressure on yourself to keep doing all the extra things you've always done, and build your very own success story? If you're feeling pressure to fit it all in, then now's the time to stop and look at what you do every day. Are there ways you can change your work habits to fit in the other things that are important to you, such as exercising or playing with the kids?

Pencil your personal life into your diary as mental health moments, and commit to giving yourself the break (even if it's just to clear your head). And share your strategy with your family because they can support you and even hide the work phone from you on the weekends if necessary. 'Rely on someone you trust to be your conscience', adds Metz. This person can look at your work–family plan and keep an eye on how hard you've tried to make the changes part of your day-to-day routine.

Home office hurdles

Running a small business from a home office throws up some unique hurdles when it comes to getting the work–family balance right. The Australian Government suggests you think about these four points before you decide that's definitely the way you want to go:

- Is your house the best location for your business? Think about things like your perception with your target market, storage of stock issues, and ease of access for clients or customers.

- Will local council regulations allow you to conduct your type of business from home? Check with your

> local council to see what sort of businesses they'll allow in certain areas.
>
> ☐ Are there any legal obligations you need to be mindful of? Things like public liability insurance can be costly (for more legal bits to be aware of, see question 40).
>
> ☐ Will your home-based business allow you to balance your work and private life? If you have children, is there space between your office and living areas? Can you close the door? Will your business be scattered over the dining room table when guests arrive?
>
> Source: <www.business.gov.au>.

Knowing when to say no

Small businesses are often set up on the premise that you'll provide better customer service than other larger businesses. With this comes being contactable and having a personal relationship with clients. 'The important thing is to create boundaries between work and your private life', says Metz. Unfortunately, thanks to technology, you're in a business environment where clients and customers often expect you to be contactable all hours of the day and night.

What you have to do is think about whether your customers really need 24-hour, seven-days-a-week access to your business and to you. If they do, one idea is to have separate phone lines for work and home, and make your home line a silent number. 'Some customers have a high level of entitlement', adds Metz. 'In this case, be aware of technology and how it dilutes these boundaries.'

She also suggests making technology work for you. Always utilise out-of-the-office messages on your phone and email when you want to be off duty. 'People have grown used to immediate responses to their needs and wants. That's why it's important to leave the message that if this can wait till Monday, they should leave a message and you'll attend to their enquiry then.' You can add that for urgent enquiries, customers should use a different number. Then if you want the weekend or night off, you can give the work mobile to one of your staff and pay them to be on call. If you're taking the phone yourself, you should still let the calls, emails or internet enquiries go through to the keeper and attend to them when you're ready, after you've done the other things you'd planned on doing.

Taking a break

Just because you own a small business doesn't mean you can't take a break. Again, it varies from person to person on how often you need to get away from work. Still, everyone needs some down time, both mentally and physically, no matter how much you love what you do. Associate Professor Isabel Metz thinks the key is in understanding what makes you tick. 'For example, if you're a Type A personality who finds it hard to dissociate yourself from work, have someone else in the family or a friend organise a holiday', she says.

Advise your customers well in advance that you're going to take this time. Giving them a good amount of warning is not only good for your customers — they may need to plan for the time when you're not contactable — but it helps you to plan and schedule things to get them done before you go away. If it's a big trip you're planning, send letters out to clients so they know who they can contact while you're away. 'People are very understanding because everyone needs to take breaks', adds Metz. 'You will not lose customers.'

49 Question: *I won't be able to do this forever: how do I start a succession plan?*

Answer: *Start with the end firmly in your sights.*

Thinking about a succession strategy for your business is a bit like trying to plan your child's 21st party the moment they're born. Unless you've been running your business for a long time and retirement is around the corner, it just seems like a waste of energy at this point. The trouble is you'll probably never get around to it. More than 60 per cent of small business owners and up to 78 per cent of family business owners have no succession plan for their businesses, according to research by Professor Beth Walker, director of the Small and Medium Enterprise Research Centre (SMERC) at Edith Cowan University. 'It's very important for small business owners to understand the impact that the lack of a succession plan can have, not only on the business but on their own expectations', she says.

What are succession plans?

A succession plan is your exit strategy if you are planning on passing control to somebody else rather than simply closing down. 'Nobody likes to think about it, but it's inevitable that one day you will leave your business', states the Australian Government's business portal <www.business. gov.au>. Whether you're thinking of selling your business (question 50), retiring (start thinking about D-day three to five years out) or you get sick and have to get out, it will give you peace of mind if you've got a plan for that day. Basically, its thinking about who'll take the reins. Business Victoria <www.business.vic.gov.au> states that there are two types of succession strategies: family plans which 'can incorporate business trusts, gifting, sale or part sale to family members'; and non-family succession plans which 'can involve full or part sale to minority or employee owners or alternatively be an open market sale'.

The plan's importance

When the day comes and you've had enough, what happens to the business you've built? Wouldn't you like it to continue to thrive? 'The numbers show us that more than half of small business owners (57 per cent) will be retiring over the next 10 years', says Professor Walker. 'Without a succession plan in place, many of those businesses will close down — and when you consider that the small and medium enterprise (SME) sector employs 48 per cent of Australia's workforce, and contributes more than 40 per cent of the country's GDP, the implications of that lack of planning are obviously far-reaching.'

The NSW Business Chamber <www.nswbusinesschamber. com.au> estimates that the life cycle of a typical private business is around 24 years. And according to Professor Walker's research, half of small business owners say that their business will be their main source of retirement funding, 'whether from a lump sum or an income stream. But if they haven't planned for a successful exit from their business, there's no guarantee that funding will be there', she says.

What to put in a plan

Every business is different, and so is every succession plan. Still, there are some common themes worth considering:

→ *Who can take over?* 'If you have children, ask yourself if they really want to come in to the business, and if they are competent enough to take over', says Dr Graham Godbee of the Macquarie Graduate School of Management. What about staff: could they take over? If you have a partner, will he or she want to run things alone? And if the business is just you, have you built it up with systems and processes so that you have a saleable commodity (not just your intellectual property) when you've had enough? 'The thing to remember is that you should be trying to maximise your return regardless of who you are thinking about in your succession plan', Godbee says.

→ *What skills will be needed?* Once you've identified who could take over your business, look at what skills this person currently has, and what he or she will need to learn before you leave. Start the training and mentoring now (see question 22). 'Do they have the right attitude, intelligence and want to learn and listen to people?' Godbee asks. As long as your chosen person has these qualities, the other skills can be learned along the way.

→ *How will it happen?* If one of your children or a staff member could take over from you, you need to think about when it will happen. Set the timetable. Write down the sort of training needed along the way to make the transition smoother. Then, make sure you communicate your plan so that everyone (including other staff) knows it's something you're working towards. And don't forget to work out how you'll let go: will you slowly phase yourself out of the operation, or leave with a big bang?

Valuing your business

The process of putting together a succession plan leads you to the question of how much your business is worth. Have you got the processes in place (from staff appraisals to customer databases to business forecasts)? Could someone step straight in and run things if you weren't there? All these things will give your business more value in the eyes of someone else. Once you work out an estimated value (see how to do this in question 50), the next step is to think about whether your successors will be able to afford to pay you out. If the answer's no, you can try together to work out ways to make it happen. Graham Godbee suggests considering vendor finance, for example, if your successor is one of your children or a loyal staff member.

Get some help

When you're pulling together a succession plan, it's important that you're in control of the process. Get the best advice you can. There are so many things to think of that it's definitely worthwhile getting a professional to look over your plan and steer you in the right direction. A business broker can give you advice on what your business is worth; your solicitor or lawyer can go through the legalities of the handover and put things in place to legally protect both you and your successor; an insurance broker can get you sorted in case ill health (or death) is the reason you will be leaving the business; and your accountant can pull all the financials together as well as keep an eye on the tax implications for everyone involved.

Online succession plan tools

There is a tonne of information on the internet about succession plans. Business Victoria (run by the Victorian Government's Department of Innovation, Industry and Regional Development) has a comprehensive succession plan section on its website <www.business.vic.gov.au>; click on 'Starting & Managing a Business', then 'Selling, Closing and Change Management', then 'Succession Planning'. Here you'll find all the information you're after, plus a Succession Plan Template to get you started.

50 **Question:** *I'm seriously thinking about selling my business. Is there a 'best time'?*

Answer: *The best time is when you've planned for the sale.*

Starting your small business and exiting it seem like polar opposites. But in fact they're really not so different. They both involve seizing opportunities. They both involve putting yourself out of your comfort zone. And they both require you to have done some planning for things to work out as well as you want. One of the big differences, though, is that by the time you're seriously thinking about selling your business, you know how much blood, sweat and tears you've ploughed in to your enterprise. And you'd like to get something for it. As much as you can, actually.

Time's right

Having someone knock on your door and make you an offer is the stuff of small business legends. In most cases, however, it's you, the owner, who decides it's time to sell. Maybe you're around the corner from retirement: according to the latest Australian Bureau of Statistics numbers, 33 per cent of Australia's small business owners are aged over 50 years old (the majority are aged between 30 and 50, at 58 per cent; and only 9 per cent are under 30 years old). Maybe ill health has sped up your selling decision. Or maybe you've had your fun and it's just time to do something different. In all these scenarios it'll work out in your favour if you're selling your business before you need to. That way it happens on your terms. How much you get for it, though, will depend on how organised you are, how well you've planned for it, and how much time you have to find the right buyer who's prepared to pay that elusive 'right' price.

What's your business worth?

This is the sixty-four-million-dollar question! And it's the one so many businesses struggle with. If you ask an accountant to value your business, they go straight to your balance sheet to look at your cash, stock and assets. They may also use industry standards to value business specifics such as your future orders. By using these calculations your accountant will come up with a number (the net asset value). It's usually below what you imagined your business to be worth. You would also factor in the time you've spent on your business, and the reputation you've achieved. Dr Graham Godbee, of the Macquarie Graduate School of Management, says that a business *is* more than a few black-and-white calculations: it's also its staff, customers, market position and reputation. 'However, it is difficult to show customer loyalty or market position or valued workers on a balance sheet (at least since slavery was fortunately abolished).'

The extra money you want for your business (over and above the net assets) is referred to in a valuation as the goodwill. It's the fuzzy component: the compensation someone is willing to give you for the 'superior future earnings potential of the acquired business', says Godbee. It's your intellectual property and the outstanding brand you've built all rolled into one. However, beauty is always in the eyes of the beholder, and at the end of the day your business is only worth what a reasonable person would pay for it.

Getting it sorted

So take a step back from your business and look at it as a stranger would. How would they perceive the value? Do you have rock solid systems in place so that anyone could step in and run things tomorrow? Or is much of the business's operational and directional brilliance locked in your head? If you haven't put anything on paper, including a business plan and forecasts for your future, how do you expect someone else to see the potential? Start with the basics such as a business plan (see question 6), including sales and profit forecasts, and get your management systems sorted. Why would someone pay top dollar for something they can't see? You'll get more for your business if a buyer can see how easily they can replicate your processes to achieve the same results you have.

Many franchises have made this an art form (as you've discovered from question 46). Some people willingly pay millions to be able to buy their tried and tested formulas (the processes and systems) and apply them to achieve their own success. Yet the idea is the same whether you're a franchise or an independent small business. Obviously it's better to have set these systems up properly from the start, but it's never too late. And if you are really serious about selling your business, it's imperative that you get it all sorted now.

Action idea: 'selling a business' checklist

When you're in the market to sell your business, there are lots of other things to organise apart from the price you're prepared to accept. The Australian Taxation Office <www.ato.gov.au> has a Selling or Closing a Business Checklist which covers many of your obligations, from how to cancel your ABN through to lodging the final tax return for your business (click on 'selling real estate, shares or your business' under 'Your business situation').

The Queensland Department of Employment, Economic Development and Innovation <www.business.qld.gov.au> also has a really useful Seller's Checklist. Although some of the information is state specific, it does list some of the other obligations you mightn't have thought of during the sale process, such as notifying WorkCover, and whether or not you want to retain any trademarks (click on 'Seller's checklist' under 'Selling or leaving').

Setting up a sale

The easiest way to sell your business is to make a proposal to someone who knows your business intimately. Succession planning (see question 49) can take a lot of the angst out of trying to find a buyer. However, if you've already gone through this process and couldn't find anyone to take over your business, you've got no choice but to look further afield. If you're a sole trader, or your partner has already exited the business, you might think you have to advertise your business for sale. Putting a classified ad in a trade or business for sale magazine or using a business broker might get you some bites (you'll find business brokers listed in the *Yellow Pages*).

A better way to pinpoint a buyer is to use your networks. Think about who would pay a premium for your business and do some targeted marketing. Graham Godbee suggests first going to your major supplier. They know how well your business is run and how much potential it has through their dealings with you. So see if they're interested in your business, or would be in the future. 'If you go to them with a plan, it increases your chances', he says.

Other networks to target include business associates from non-competing industries. Or, if you're ready for it, you could also let your competition (particularly friendly competitors) know you may be in the market to sell your business at some time in the future. In every conversation you have around the idea of selling your business, it's up to you to give the prospective buyer an overwhelming sense that it's a worthwhile investment: they too will be as big a success as you!

Appendix:
Writing a business plan

A business plan is basically a summary of why you are in business, how you run things, your product and your customers. It really can be as short or as long as you want; however, the best advice is to keep it clear and concise. You can cover things such as the background to your business, your objectives, a market and competitor analysis, a marketing plan, an operational plan, a financial plan and a human resources plan. The list of headings and questions here is a guide to writing a basic business plan. If you want to add more things, even better.

The more questions you can ask of yourself and your business and the more details you can summarise into your business plan, the stronger it will be. You will then have all your information in one easily accessible document, and you'll be able to plan in a more strategic way. But just remember: it's not necessarily the words you write down but the thought process you go through that makes this exercise worthwhile for every small business. A business plan will help you articulate your vision and help you manage and plan your next moves. You'll also need all of the following information written down if you ever want to approach a bank or external investor to talk to them about investing in your business. The other key thing to remember is to review it regularly (every six to 12 months) so that you have an idea of how you're tracking against your plan, and what needs to be changed so you can generate even more success.

Executive summary

Write this executive summary after you've completed your business plan. This part of the document is where you encapsulate all the things you've discovered about your business, your team, your product or service and your customers, and how all the elements of your plan point towards your vision. Outline your potential for growth, the reasons you think you'll be successful and your financial forecasts (this overview can be an important summary for investors and financiers to look at and assess). The whole executive summary shouldn't be any more than a page in length.

Business purpose

Take a good long look at all the ideas that will propel your business success.

→ What's driven you to open your own small business and what's your business trying to achieve?

→ What's your philosophy? You can even include your professional and personal goals: the things that will underpin what you do and how you do it.

Business opportunity

Analyse some of the historical trends in your industry over the past five to 10 years.

→ Where are the gaps in the market?

→ Why do you believe you could fill them with your product or service?

→ How do you think you'll do this?

Business concept

This is more about the machinations of your organisation, and the role they play in bringing your concept to life.

→ How have you structured your business, and why?

→ What are your company details (location, ABN, contact details) and how have you set things up financially?

→ Will the talents of your management team (even if it's just you) drive your success?

→ How will these key skills benefit your business? (You can list the qualifications of you as the founder and your senior people.)

→ What's the scope of your business (local, national, international)?

→ What are the short- and long-term objectives of your business?

Market analysis

If you regularly review this part of your business plan, you'll always have your finger on the pulse of your sector.

→ How big is your industry? Do some research (industry associations are often a good place to start) to find out the trends and growth potential of the industry.

→ Who are your customers (include their age, sex, income levels and any defining lifestyle identifiers) and where do they live?

→ Are they currently having their needs met in your market?

→ What do they think of your competitors?

→ Who are your competitors (direct and indirect) and how are they performing?

Marketing plan

As part of the marketing plan section, put together a SWOT analysis (strengths, weaknesses, opportunities and threats). This will help you work out how you will get the most mileage out of your strengths and every opportunity, and how you will minimise the effects of your weaknesses and any threats. (For more on doing a SWOT analysis for your business, see question 6.) Then you can write down your marketing objectives.

→ What are the unique and innovative features of your product or service?

→ How can you translate these into a competitive advantage in your marketplace?

→ How much does the price of products in this market affect purchasing habits?

→ What effect will this have on the price of your offering? Is there anything else that affects people's willingness to buy in your market?

→ Would people be willing to change from the companies they currently purchase from?

→ How will you get your message to them: what sort of advertising and promotions (for example, flyers, mainstream media, social media) do you want to implement over the next year, and what do you hope to achieve out of them?

→ How much will this planned activity cost?

Business development

Set some development targets and then balance these with how you will make them happen, taking into consideration your current (and future) production capabilities.

→ How do you plan to develop your product or service, and how much time and money will it take?

→ What are the things that could thwart your plans?

→ What sort of insurances will help mitigate your risks, and how much will these cost? (For some tips, go to question 36.)

→ Do you need to get any government approvals or permits to run your business?

→ Do you have to register for GST?

Production plan

When it comes to production, it helps to briefly explain all your production processes. This is your chance to really look at the engine room of your enterprise.

→ What's your production capacity on a monthly basis?

→ How much lead time do you need to gather supplies and fill orders?

→ How flexible is your production capacity if a big order comes in?

→ What about your plant and machinery needs: what are the time frames if something has to be replaced? Could this impact your production?

→ Have you thought about quality control? Do you have the procedures in place to make sure your product or service is great every time?

→ Are your distribution channels up to scratch?

Financial plan

Take the time to write down a financial map of your business. It's an essential element if you ever contemplate seeking out finance of some sort. And attach a current copy of your balance sheet projections and a cash flow forecast (see more of this in question 10) to the business plan so that you (or anyone else) can see at a glance how your business is performing.

→ Where do you plan to get your funds for your business, regardless of whether you're in the set-up, stabilisation or growth phases?

→ What are your existing loans and liabilities?

→ How much debt are you prepared to go into, and how are any repayments going to be supported by your cash flow?

→ What sorts of systems and procedures do you have in place that can monitor your cash flow?

Growth and contingency plans

While a crystal ball would be nice to have, these growth and contingency plans will have to suffice!

→ What's your strategy for growth (listing as many of the elements involved)?

→ How many and what types of resources could (and should) you throw into this growth?

→ What are your contingency plans when it comes to dealing with problems that may arise with your market or your finances?

Appendices

1   Include all supporting documents (such as your business registration) with your business plan.

2   Attach any additional breakdowns of your analyses.

3   Include a high-level budget.

Glossary

ABN Australian Business Number; an 11-digit number that allows businesses to identify themselves.

ABR Australian Business Register; records the information from companies when they register for an ABN.

ABS Australian Bureau of Statistics; a federal government agency that collects data from Australian Census and other sources.

accrual accounting This is when you put your revenues alongside your expenses over a particular time frame.

alternative dispute resolution Includes mediation, arbitration, conciliation and counselling as alternatives to going to court.

anchor tenant Another business, such as a supermarket, that draws people to the complex in which you might be renting your retail premises.

ASIC Australian Securities & Investments Commission.

assets   Those things which you own.

ATO   Australian Taxation Office.

Austrade   Australian Government's trade commission.

balance sheet   An outline of your assets and your liabilities.

BAS   Business Activity Statement; the single statement the Australian Taxation Office requires you to fill out regularly when you are registered for GST.

BEC   Business Enterprise Centre.

blogs   A social media tool where you publish or 'post' your own online content.

business angels   Private backers who are matched with small businesses and provide them with funds and expertise for a financial return.

business plan   A document that lists your business goals, and how you think you'll achieve them.

capital expenses   Major equipment or machinery expenses.

carbon footprint   The amount of greenhouse gases you produce through your daily business and personal activities.

cash accounting   Keeping track of when cash comes in and out of a business from your sales and expenses.

cash burn rate   How much cash it would take to keep your business operating if no new cash came in.

cash flow   The amount of money that comes in and goes out of your business.

cash flow forecast   How much cash — petty cash and cash in the bank — your business has access to and how much cash it takes to keep your business actually operating on a daily or weekly basis.

channel partners   Other businesses your customers (or potentials) patronise; you might be able to cross-sell your services with these businesses.

choice liability   The penalty you incur from the Australian Taxation Office if you pay an employee's superannuation into the wrong fund.

coach   Someone who assists you in a specific task or skill and follows up to make sure it's happened.

Codes of Practice   The standards of conduct that are expected of businesses in Australia. From having to have clean staff toilets to alerting staff to the dangers of handling hazardous substances, the industry codes cover just about every health and safety area in your workplace.

commercial feasibility   Whether your business ideas will make money.

conversion ratio   The percentage of leads (customer enquiries) converted to sales.

conversion time   The time between the call and the sale.

current assets   Assets you expect to convert into cash in the next 12 months, including cash, accounts receivable, inventory (stock) and prepayments.

current liabilities   Liabilities you will have to pay for in the next 12 months, including bank loans, business credit cards and overdrafts, accounts payable to creditors, income and PAYG tax payable, GST liabilities, and other accrued expenses.

customer relationship management (CRM) system
A computer-based application that captures information about your customers.

debt   An amount of money you borrow from a bank or lending institution.

direct discrimination   Treating one person less favourably than another because of particular attributes such as race, sex, age or religion.

direct mail campaigns   A traditional marketing tool where you buy a list or database of prospective names and then get information about your business directly into people's hands.

diversification   Selling products and services you've never dealt with and that are unfamiliar to your customers.

domain name   The online location or identifying address of your website.

elevator pitch   What you say to get a person interested in your product or service in a short time (the time it takes to get in an elevator and get to another floor).

employee awards   Stipulate the terms of minimum pay, maximum working hours, holiday and sick leave entitlements and long service leave, among other things; they are legally binding.

equity   The part of your company — a share — that you own. Because you own it, you can give up some of your equity to raise funds for your business.

e-Record   The Australian Taxation Office's free electronic record-keeping package to help you maintain accurate records and stay up to date with your tax obligations.

export plan   Should include information on target markets, time frames for production and delivery, customs duties and any overseas marketing strategies.

Fair Dismissal Code   Provides employers and employees with a fair and reasonable process of sorting out any workplace issue that might end in dismissal.

fair trading   You are legally bound by federal, state and territory legislation to conduct your trade in a fair and efficient way.

Fair Work Australia   Acts as the 'independent umpire' to help sort out disputes in the workplace.

FBT   You're obliged to pay fringe benefits tax if you give your employees or their families benefits above and beyond their salary and wages. Examples of benefits include a car, car parking, low interest loans and payments of private expenses.

financial risk   Includes commitments such as debt, long-term leases, insurance cover and the hedging you do on things such as exchange rates.

firewall   A software system that aims to limit who can get into your computer.

fully drawn advance   A bank loan facility that is secured against residential or commercial property.

GIC   General Interest Charge; the penalty for not completing your BAS on time.

goodwill   The compensation someone is willing to give you for the reputation and contacts of the acquired business (over and above the net assets).

GST   Goods and services tax; the value-added tax of 10 per cent that is placed on most goods and services produced in Australia.

income statement   A summary of your business transactions for a set period (say, a year) that lead to a profit or loss for the business ('what we sold and what it cost us').

indirect discrimination   Treating everyone the same but in a way that is unfair to one or more people; for example, where the design of a workplace prevents a person with a disability from accessing equipment necessary to do the job.

intellectual property (IP)   Relates to the confidential information that was used to create or continues to drive your small business.

internet service provider (ISP)   A company that connects you to the internet.

leverage (or gearing)   The use of debt (borrowings) to bolster returns (for example, a 10 per cent deposit on a factory and the rest borrowed from the bank).

liabilities   The amounts which you owe other people.

liability insurance   Cover in case your product or professional services cause a third party death or injury, loss or damage of property or financial loss resulting from your negligence.

line of credit   A pre-approved amount of credit to a specified limit (similar to a credit card). It's also known as a revolving line of credit because you can continually make withdrawals and pay back the amounts down to the credit limit. A line of credit is normally secured against assets.

loans   Finance (usually for a certain term or time frame) for when the money you need in your business is for longer term needs.

market development   You take your existing product or service to new markets.

marketing   Getting a message out about your brand, doing research and finding out what motivates your target market.

market intelligence data   What your customers are really thinking. Measure and report on it so you can try to predict how your market will act.

market penetration   When you either grow the volume within your current market or you start to snare market share off competitors.

market research   Is all about getting answers. Does a particular group of people need a particular product or service? Would they pay money for it? How much would they pay? For start-up businesses, ask questions such as what size is your market? For existing small businesses, how can you keep your eyes open, and maintain your competitive edge?

mentor   Someone who guides you through your professional growth. Mentoring is about creating an atmosphere of advice and support in your business.

micro business   Those businesses that employ up to four people.

networking   Talking to people with the aim of picking up general or more specific market intelligence that could benefit your business.

non-current (or fixed) assets   Assets that won't be converted into cash in the next 12 months, including buildings and land owned by the business, plant and equipment, office equipment and motor vehicles, plus other assets such as investments and goodwill.

non-current liabilities   Liabilities that don't need to be paid in the next 12 months, including mortgages, lease payments and provisions for employee entitlements.

occupational health and safety (OH&S)   It's about having a systematic approach to preventing death, injury and disease in your workplace.

operational risk   The things that can go wrong in your business that you mightn't have control over, including competitor activity, equipment breakdown and default by a major customer.

outsourcing   Paying other people or businesses to do specific tasks for your business.

overdrafts   A short-term finance facility that can prop up your business when your seasonal cash flow is low (for example, for two or three months of the year), or so you can buy that piece of equipment that will help you generate more money for your business.

overtrading   When you grow sales quickly, and your business doesn't have the additional cash to fund an increase in assets to support the boom.

partnerships   You have someone else along for the ride, sharing the costs, celebrating the successes and commiserating the losses.

PAYG   Pay As You Go instalments allow you to make down payments towards your end-of-year income tax liability.

PAYG tax withheld   The PAYG tax amounts that you must withhold from your employees, contractors, company directors if you have them, or other businesses that don't give you their ABN on invoices.

PayPal   An international payments system that lets you or your customers send money safely over the internet.

performance appraisals   Specific goals, targets and what employees have done well written into a document that's annually reviewed.

phishing   When you're tricked into giving your personal or banking and finance details that are then used to illegitimately tap into your bank accounts.

point of sale (POS) integration systems   A system that's hooked up to your cash register (point of sale) that tracks where customers are from, how much each customer spends and what they buy.

profit   Your revenues minus your expenses.

proprietary limited companies   A structure whereby a business is registered as a legal company entity (through ASIC), and liability is limited to the business, not the proprietor or the shareholders.

return on equity   The amount of money an investor should be able to expect from loaning you money. Return on equity = net profit after tax ÷ shareholders funds.

revenue   Income including sales, fees earned, rent and interest earned.

RSS feeds   Rich Site Summary or Really Simple Syndication; it keeps you up to date with any new content from your favourite websites and blogs.

search engine optimisation (SEO)   How you get your website to be ranked as highly as possible when people search for information over the internet. Your aim is to have your business site ranked at number one on the first page of a Google search for your primary keyword or keywords.

shareholders   They own a share (a financial portion) of a company.

small business   A business with fewer than 20 employees.

social media   An ever-growing array of web-based tools to help people create online networks.

sole trader   An individual trading on his or her own.

SSL (Secure Socket Layer protocol) Certificates   Encrypts information on your site so that when people enter their personal details, their information won't be shared around on the world wide web.

superannuation   There's a legislative requirement that you pay money (known as the superannuation guarantee) into a registered superannuation fund for almost all employees as a way of helping them save for their retirement.

superannuation guarantee charge   The Australian Taxation Office penalty you are charged for not paying enough of your super obligations.

sustainable growth rate   A short-hand approximation of cash flow availability as a company changes its sales levels. The Sales Growth formula is (Return On Assets × (1 − dividends)) ÷ (Equity ÷ Assets − (Return On Assets) × (1 − dividends)).

SWOT   Stands for strengths (the advantages you have over your competitors), weaknesses (what you could improve), opportunities (the areas that offer the best chance of growth) and threats (the obstacles you face, either within your business or from your competitors).

tax enquiry   An examination of your tax affairs to see whether you've done what is required of you under the tax laws.

tax file number   A number you or your business is issued with by the Australian Taxation Office when you start to earn an income or access government payments.

trust   A legal structure where an entity has the responsibility of holding property or income for the benefit of others (known as the trust's beneficiaries).

venture capitalists   Investors who are prepared to risk their own money in a business embarking on expansion, new technology or research and development, in return for a share in the company or other financial returns.

vicarious liability   You are legally bound by Commonwealth anti-discrimination laws. When you have taken 'all reasonable steps' to reduce your liability for discrimination and harassment in your workplace, you may come under vicarious liability provisions of the legislation (that is, your legal liability is limited).

workers' compensation   Part of the OH&S laws; requires injured workers to have access to first aid, monetary compensation while they're recuperating and a return-to-work rehabilitation program.

Useful websites

Government

Each of the following federal, state and territory government websites has specific small business sections:

<www.abs.gov.au> The Australian Bureau of Statistics is a great source of market information.

<www.accc.gov.au> The Australian Competition and Consumer Commission's site. Check out *The Little Black Book of Scams* under 'Publications'.

<www.acma.gov.au> The Australian Communications and Media Authority has what's new in online communication.

<www.asic.gov.au> Australian Securities & Investments Commission.

<www.ato.gov.au> The Australian Taxation Office site is a must-look for everyone in small business.

<www.ausindustry.gov.au> AusIndustry is a federal government initiative.

<www.austrade.gov.au>   Austrade has export tips and networking events.

<www.business.gov.au>   Australian Government business portal is the best place to start as it has good basic information across myriad areas and links to many other government sites for easy-to-use templates.

<www.business.qld.gov.au>   The Queensland Government's Department of Employment, Industry Development and Innovation has created this specific Smart Skills website which has many online diagnostic tools.

<www.business.vic.gov.au>   Business Victoria, which is an arm of the Department of Innovation, Industry and Regional Development, has great small business specific information.

<www.climatechange.gov.au>   The federal government's Department of Climate Change has a 'Business & Industry' section outlining climate change programs that might be relevant to your business.

<www.consumer.gov.au>   NSW Department of Fair Trading.

<www.customs.gov.au>   Australian Customs Service, for anyone looking at importing or exporting.

<www.deewr.gov.au>   The federal government's Department of Education, Employment and Workplace Relations has essential workplace information.

<www.development.tas.gov.au>   Tasmanian Department of Economic Development, Tourism and the Arts offers handy templates.

<www.e-businessguide.gov.au>   Department of Broadband, Communications and the Digital Economy's e-business guide.

<www.efic.gov.au>   The Export Finance and Insurance Corporation (EFIC).

<www.environment.gov.au> The federal government's Department of the Environment, Water, Heritage and the Arts.

<www.eowa.gov.au> The Equal Opportunity for Women in the Workplace Agency (EOWA).

<www.fairtrading.qld.gov.au> Queensland Office of Fair Trading.

<www.fairwork.gov.au> The Australian Government's Fair Work Online website has lots of tips for business owners.

<www.grantslink.gov.au> GrantsLINK is an initiative of the federal government's Department of Infrastructure, Transport, Regional Development and Local Government, which lists all the government grants available to the private sector.

<www.hreoc.gov.au> The Human Rights and Equal Opportunity Commission has tips on fair human resources management.

<www.innovation.gov.au> The federal government's Department of Innovation, Industry, Science and Research. Aimed more at R&D but worth a look.

<www.nt.gov.au/business> Northern Territory Department of Business and Employment; also has easy-to-use templates.

<www.ntis.gov.au> The National Training Information Service.

<www.privacy.gov.au> Office of the Privacy Commissioner is worth a look if you're selling online.

<www.ret.gov.au> The federal government's Department of Resources, Energy and Tourism.

<www.scamwatch.gov.au> The Australian Competition and Consumer Commission's SCAMwatch site will help you protect your business.

<http://sd.qld.gov.au> The Queensland Government's Department of Employment, Industry Development and Innovation.

<www.smallbiz.nsw.gov.au> The Small Business Development Corporation (sponsored by the NSW Department of State and Regional Development).

<www.training.com.au> The federal government's training portal.

<www.treasury.gov.au> This site includes the federal Treasury's e-commerce checklist.

Finance

Here are some of the best sites to access for general finance information. You also should check specifics relating to your business with your accountant.

<www.anz.com/small-business> ANZ Bank's small business portal.

<www.bankers.asn.au> The Australian Bankers' Association.

<www.cpaaustralia.com.au> CPA Australia.

<www.expensereduction.com> Expense Reduction Analysts.

<www.fido.asic.gov.au> The Australian Securities & Investments Commission's consumer and business information site.

<www.hrblock.com.au> H&R Block, respected tax accountants with offices nationally.

<www.lifewise.org.au> Investment and Financial Services Association's (IFSA) site Lifewise.

<www.niba.com.au> The National Insurance Brokers Association.

<www.smallbusinessbanking.com.au> The Small Business Banking Portal from the Australian Bankers' Association.

<www.westpac.com.au> Go to the 'Business Banking' section of Westpac's site.

Legal information

These legal information sites are a useful guide; however, it's always worth passing legal questions by your solicitor or lawyer.

<www.artslaw.com.au> The Arts Law Centre of Australia.

<www.auscert.org.au> The Australian Computer Emergency Response Team (AusCERT).

<www.deir.qld.gov.au/workplace/index.htm> Queensland's Department of Employment and Industrial Relations — Workplace Health and Safety.

<www.ipaustralia.gov.au> IP Australia's Smart Start site.

<www.legalaccess.com.au> Legal Access Services.

<www.protectfinancialid.org.au> The Protect Your Financial Identity site, which has been put together by the Australian Bankers' Association, Australian High Tech Crime Centre and the Australian Securities & Investments Commission.

<www.safeworkaustralia.gov.au> Safe Work Australia.

<www.safework.sa.gov.au> SafeWork SA.

<http://sblegal.innovation.gov.au> The Department of Innovation, Industry, Science and Research's dedicated Small Business Legal Issues website.

<www.workcover.act.gov.au> Australian Capital Territory's Office of Regulatory Services (ORS) WorkCover.

<www.workcover.nsw.gov.au> WorkCover NSW.

<www.workcover.tas.gov.au>   WorkCover Tasmania.

<www.workcover.vic.gov.au>   WorkSafe Victoria.

<www.worksafe.nt.gov.au>   NT WorkSafe.

<www.worksafe.wa.gov.au>   WorkSafe WA.

Business

There is a raft of online information targeted at small business owners. Here are some of the best sites I found.

<www.acci.asn.au>   The Australian Chamber of Commerce and Industry (ACCI).

<www.aigroup.asn.au>   The Australian Industry Group.

<www.beca.org.au>   Business Enterprise Centre Australia.

<www.carnegiemg.com.au>   Carnegie Management Group, for business coaching and mentoring services.

<www.mentoring-australia.org>   The link to Mentoring Australia.

<www.nswbusinesschamber.com.au>   The NSW Chamber of Commerce.

<www.sbms.org.au>   The Small Business Mentoring Service.

<www.terris.com.au>   Check the resources section of Terris Business Consultants.

Marketing

Learn how to target your market and get the biggest bang from your marketing buck from these marketing-focused websites.

<www.about.sensis.com.au/small_business>   *Small Business, Big Opportunity*, produced by leading Australian information providers Sensis.

<www.advertisingstandardsbureau.com.au>   Advertising Standards Bureau.

<www.auspostbusiness.com.au/Marketing-Your-Business> One of Australia Post's services to small business.

<www.chilliwebsites.com>   Create your own website.

<www.commoncraft.com/socialmedia>   *Social Media in Plain English* site.

<www.ducttapemarketing.com>   This site includes a link to the e-book *Let's Talk: social media for small business* by John Jantsch of Duct Tape Marketing.

<www.homestead.com>   Create your own website.

<www.marketingangels.com.au>   Marketing Angels.

<www.microsoft.com/smallbusiness/resources/marketing> Information from the Microsoft Small Business Centre.

<www.pria.com.au>   The Public Relations Institute of Australia has a list of PR consultants in your state.

<www.startlocal.com.au>   Start Local, Australia's local search engine and business directory.

<www.typepad.com>   TypePad website creation homepage.

<www.webindustry.com.au>   Australian Web Industry Association.

<http://wipa.org.au/>   The Web Industry Professionals Association.

<www.wordpress.org>   WordPress website creation homepage.

<www.wordsthatsell.com.au>   Words that Sell.

<www.zdnet.com.au>   ZDNet Australia website with information on all things online.

Other information

Here are some additional websites I found useful during my research for other areas that affect small business.

<www.aqis.gov.au>   The Australian Quarantine and Inspection Service (AQIS).

<www.business.ecu.edu.au/schools/man/smerc/green-advantage>   The Small and Medium Enterprise Research Centre (SMERC) at Edith Cowan University in Western Australia.

<www.carbonneutral.com/business-carbon-calculator> The Carbon Neutral Business Carbon Calculator.

<www.climatepositive.org/measure>   Climate Positive has a Small Business Calculator at this link.

<www.franchise.org.au>   Franchise Council of Australia.

<www.greenbizcheck.com>   GreenBizCheck.

<www.humanmetrics.com>   Discover your personality type.

<www.redcross.org.au>   Australian Red Cross.

<www.wishlist.com.au>   Wish List: corporate gifts.

Index